God's Promises and Assurances

By

Cecilia D. Porter

Contents

- Trusting In God's Promises And His Truth..................1
- Rewards In Heaven..................5
- Strength..................9
- Eternal Life..................17
- Righteous And Righteousness..................23
- Provision..................30
- Trust..................37
- His Plans For US..................42
- Healing Physical, Emotional, And Spiritually..................52
- Salvation..................58
- Faith, Faithful, And Faithfulness..................64
- Peace And Comfort..................72
- Wisdom..................79
- Joy..................87
- Love..................98
- Shelter And Refuge..................108
- Deliverance From Evil..................114

TABLE OF CONTENTS

- Trouble 120
- Prayer 128
- Secrets And Mysteries 137
- Hope 147
- Help And Guidance 157
- Protection 162

Trusting In God's Promises And His Truth

The Bible has so many promises in it. God is the God of promises. By faith, you must trust the promises of God. When God makes a promise, you better believe it will be fulfilled. You have to wait for them by faith. You wait for them in hope. You wait for them in patience. You wait for them in anticipation. You wait for them in expectation. You may have to wait while in sorrow. You may have to painfully wait. And yet, you just wait.

Abraham waited for God's promise for more that 20 years. He describes it as, "him who had the promises." God promised Abraham and Sarah that from them would rise a great nation. He promised them a child at the age of 100 and 90, respectfully. The Lord kept His promise.

The Lord promised Noah and his descendants that He would never destroy the world again with a universal flood. The Lord made an everlasting covenant with Noah and his descendants, establishing the rainbow as the sign of His promise.

Joseph had to wait for over 12 years for God's promise to come to fruition. God gave him a promise in a dream. He dreamed that his brothers and his father, Jacob would bow down to him. He was sold to a band of Ishmaelites who in turn sold him as a slave to Potiphar, then thrown in prison because of a lie. Through the process of events, Joseph rose from becoming a slave to the viceroy of Egypt (the second highest in command under the king).

Moses had to wait years for God's promise. God sent Moses to organize the Israelites exodus from Egypt and give them the land of Canaan. "Therefore, say to the Israelite: 'I am the Lord, and I will bring you our from under the yoke of the Egyptians. I will free you from being slaves to them, and I will redeem you with an outstretched arm and with mighty acts of judgment. I will take you as my own people, and I will be your God. Then you will know that I am the Lord your God, who brought you out from under the yoke of the Egyptians. And I will bring you to the land I swore with uplifted hand to give to Abraham, to Isaac, and to Jacob. I will give it to you as a possession. I am the Lord." (Exodus 6:6). It was the Promised Land: the land flowing with milk and honey.

David had to wait for God's promise. David was the second King of Israel. He wanted to build a temple to worship God. God told the prophet Nathan that He would not allow David to build the temple but his son Solomon would. God promised David that his seed would sit upon his throne, as king, ruling over an everlasting Kingdom. "For unto us a child is born, unto us a son is given: and the government shall be upon his shoulder: and his name shall be called Wonderful, Counsellor, The mighty God, The everlasting

Father, The Prince of Peace. Of the increase of his government and peace there shall be no end, upon the throne of David, and upon his kingdom, to order it, and to establish it with judgment and with justice from henceforth even for ever. The zeal of the Lord of hosts will perform this." (Isaiah 9:6-7)

Jesus is the fulfillment of God's promise to send a Messiah who will bless all nations. Apostle Paul, who was God's chosen missionary to the Gentiles, said that all of God's promises find their "Yes" in Jesus. "As surely as God is faithful, our word to you does not waver betwen "Yes" and "No." For Jesus Christ, the Son of God, does not waver between "Yes" and "No." He is the one whom Silas, Timothy, and I preached to you, and as God's ultimate "Yes," he always does what he says. For all of God's promises have been fulfilled in Christ, our "Amen" (which means "Yes) ascends to God for his glory." (2 Corinthians 1:18-20)

So if you are yet waiting, then you are in very good company. God keeps His promises, even if it seems like it is just impossible. Just because there is a delay, it doesn't negate the promises of God.

For those who feed on God's promises, you will never spiritually starve or be thirsty. So many people place their hope and faith in the wrong things. Some people put their trust in their money, jobs, relationships, material possessions, and etc. But the Bible says, "Trust in the Lord with all your heart and do not lean on your own understanding. In all your ways acknowledge him, and he will make straight your paths" (Proverbs 3:5-6). All of God's promises are as solid as a rock.

As a believer, God promised forgiveness of sins. We are also promised the Holy Spirit. Jesus called the Holy Spirit "the Promise of My Father." The forgiveness of sins and the Holy Spirit are in Acts 2:38, "Then Peter said unto them, Repent, and be baptized every one of you in the name of Jesus Christ for the remission of sins, and ye shall receive the gift of the Holy Ghost." Isn't it amazing that God cannot lie! God promised us that we will be heirs in His kingdom, "Hearken, my beloved brethren. Hath not God chosen the poor of this world rich in faith, and heirs of the kingdom which he hath promised to them that love him?"

Not only do the Bible lists the promises of God, but it is the Inspired Word of God, because God divinely inspired the writers of each of the 66 Scriptural Book.

The Bible itself, is a witness of God speaking through mankind. "All Scripture is given by inspiration of God, and is profitable for doctrine, for reproof, for correction, for instruction in righteousness" (2 Timothy 3:16).

"For no prophecy was ever made by an act of human will, but men moved by the Holy Spirit spoke from God" (2 Peter 1:21). This confirms that each writer was inspired by God to write what God wanted them to write.

The Bible is a book that acts as a guideline or rule book of the do's and don'ts of life. It is a roadmap as what to do to avoid eternal damnation.

Rewards In Heaven

God's Word is full of encouragements for us to look forward to once we become heaven bound. One such encouragement is the promise of rewards. When this life's battle is over, those who diligently run the spiritual race, will receive rewards for their faithfulness at the Judgment Seat of Christ. "For we will all stand before God's judgment seat of Christ. For it is written, As I live, saith the Lord, every knee shall bow to me, and every tongue shall confess to God. So then every one of us shall give account of himself to God" (Romans 14:10-12).

We will stand before the Judgment Seat for our faithful service to Him to be evaluated and rewarded. The Judgment Seat of Christ does not determine our salvation, because we are saved by grace through our faith in Christ, and all of our sins have been forgiven.

God will give us rewards in order to fulfill the law of sowing and reaping. Jesus will share His reward with us, because we are heirs of God and co-heirs with Christ. Through Chirst's resurrection,

we will gain an inheritance in heaven, when our earthly story has been completed, our eternal rewards will be given to us.

"Blessed is the man that endureth temptation: for when he is tried, he shall receive the crown of life, which the Lord hath promised to them that love him." - James 1:12

"And, behold, I come quickly; and my reward is with me, to give every man according as his work shall be." - Revelation 22:12

"Fear none of those things which thou shalt suffer: behold, the devil shall cast some of you into prison, that ye may be tried; and ye shall have tribulation ten days: be thou faithful unto death, and I will give thee a crown of life." - Revelation 2:10

"For the Son of man shall come in the glory of his Father with his angels; and then he shall reward every man according to his works." - Matthew 16:27

"Rejoice, and be exceeding glad: for great is your reward in heaven: for so persecuted they the prophets which were before you." - Matthew 5:12

"Charge them that are rich in this world, that they be not high-minded, nor trust in uncertain riches, but in the living God, who giveth us richly all things to enjoy; That they do good, that they rich in good works, ready to distribute, willing to communicate; Laying up in store for themselves a good foundation against the time to come, that they may lay hold on eternal life." - 1 Timothy 6:17-19

"For we must all appear before the judgment seat of Christ; that every one may receive the things done in his body, according to that he hath done, whether it be good or bad." - 2 Corinthians 5:10

"But as it is written, Eye hath not seen, nor ear heard, neither have entered into the heart of man, the things which God hath prepared for them that love him." - 1 Corinthians 2:9

"But thou, when thou prayest, enter into thy closet, and when thou hast shut thy door, pray to thy Father which is in secret; and thy Father which seeth in secret shall reward thee openly." - Matthew 6:6

"And these shall go away into everlasting punishment: but the righteous into life eternal." - Matthew 25:46

"I the Lord search the heart, I try the reins, even to give every man according to his ways, and according to the fruit of his doings." - Jeremiah 17:10

"Now he that planteth and he that watereth are one: and every man shall receive his own reward according to his own labour." - 1 Corinthians 3:8

"Now if any man build upon this foundation gold, silver, precious stones, wood, hay, stubble; Every man's work shall be made manifest: for the day shall declare it, because it shall be revealed by fire; and the fire shall try every man's work of what sort it is. If any

man's work abide which he hath built thereupon, he shall receive a reward." - 1 Corinthians 3:12-14

"Think not that I am come to destroy the law, or the prophets: I am not come to destroy, but to fulfill. For verily I say unto you, Till heaven and earth pass, one jot or one title shall in no wise pass from the law, til all be fulfilled. Whosoever therefore shall break one of these least commandments, and shall teach men so, he shall be called the least in the kingdom of heaven: but whosoever shall do and teach them, the same shall be called great in the kingdom of heaven." - Matthew 5:17-19

"Every man's work shall be made manifest: for the day shall declare it, because it shall be revealed by fire; and the fire shall try every man's work of what sort it is. If any man's work abide which he hath built thereupon, he shall receive a reward. If any man's work shall be burned, he shall suffer loss: but he himself shall be saved; yet so as by fire." - 1 Corinthians 3:13-15

"Lay not up for yourselves treasures upon earth, where moth and rust doth corrupt, and where thieves break through and steal: But lay up for yourselves treasures in heaven, where neither moth nor rust doth corrupt, and where thieves do not break through nor steal: For where your treasure is, there will your heart be also." - Matthew 6:19-21

Strength

Everyone gets tired and grows weary. When crisis strikes, they cause us to fall apart. The moment we are confronted with trouble, we collapse with anxiety and stress. So many people are "stressed out" these days. We feel the sting of grief or pain and we questions God's presence.

God never promised us a stress-free life, absent of pain, suffering, and despair. But God did promise us that He would be our God and we His people, and He has fulfilled His promise through Jesus Christ. No matter how hard things may seem, we are never alone. When we feel weak and helpless, that is when we can feel the full power and grace of God. God is our Creator, Redeemer, Provider, Sustainer, and Friend.

God, who knitted us together while we were in our mother's womb and knows the exact numbers of hairs on our head, is always with us, every day of our lives. God has never left us and He never will. God is the source of our strength and the ever present help in time of need. "He gives power to the faint, and strengthens

the powerless." When you put your hope in Him, He will renew your strength.

"The name of the Lord is a strong tower: the righteous runneth into it, and is safe." - Proverbs 18:10

"Ah Lord God! behold, thou hast made the heaven and the earth by thy great power and stretched out arm, and there is nothing too hard for thee:" - Jeremiah 32:17

"But the salvation of the righteous is of the Lord: he is their strength in the time of trouble." - Psalm 37:39

"And Jesus looking upon them saith, With men it is impossible, but not with God: for with God all things are possible." - Mark 10:27

"Then he said unto them, Go your way, eat the fat, and drink the sweet, and send portions unto them for whom nothing is prepared: for this day is holy unto our Lord: neither be ye sorry; for the joy of the Lord is your strength." - Nehemiah 8:10

"My flesh and my heart faileth: but God is the strength of my heart, and my portion for ever." - Psalm 73:26

"The Lord is on my side; I will not fear: what can man do unto me?" - Psalm 118:6

"And thou shalt love the Lord thy God with all thine heart, and with all thy soul, and with all thy might." - Deuteronomy 6:5

"The Lord will strengthen him upon the bed of languishing: thou wilt make all his bed in his sickness." - Psalm 41:3

"I will love thee, O Lord, my strength." - Psalm 18;1

"In the day when I cried thou answeredst me, and strengthenedst me with strenght in my soul." - Psalm 138:3

"Thou in thy mercy hast led forth the people which thou hast redeemed: thou hast guided them in thy strength unto thy holy habitation." - Exodus 15:13

"God is my strength and power: and he maketh my way perfect." - 2 Samuel 22:33

"The Lord is my rock, and my fortress, and my deliverer; my God, my strength, in whom I will trust: my buckler, and the horn of my salvation, and my high tower." - Psalm 18:2

"For the eyes of the Lord run to and fro throughout the whole earth, to shew himself strong in the behalf of them whose heart is perfect toward him. Herein thou hast done foolishly: therefore from henceforth thou shalt have wars." - 2 Chronicles 16:9

"For thou hast girded me with strength to battle: them that rose up against me hast thou subdued under me." - 2 Samuel 22:40

"For when we were yet without strength, in due time Christ died for the ungodly." - Romans 5:6

"Because of his strength will I wait upon thee: for God is my defence." - Psalm 59:9

"And let us not be weary in well doing: for in due season we shall reap, if we faint not." - Galatians 6:9

"And said, O man greatly beloved, fear not: peace be unto thee, be strong, yea, be strong. And when he had spoken unto me, I was strengthened, and said, Let my lord speak; for thou hast strengthened me." - Daniel 10:19

"Confess your faults one to another, and pray one for another, that ye may be healed. The effectual fervent prayer of a righteous man availeth much." - James 5:16

"It is God that girdeth me with strength, and maketh my way perfect. He maketh my feet like hinds' feet, and setteth me upon my high places. He teacheth my hands to war, so that a bow of steel is broken by mine arms." - Psalm 18:32-34

"O God, thou art terrible out of thy holy places: the God of Israel is he that giveth strength and power unto his people. Blessed be God." - Psalm 68:35

"Wait on the Lord: be of good courage, and he shall strengthen thine heart: wait , I say on the Lord." - Psalm 27:14

"The Lord thy God in the midst of thee is mighty; he will save, he will rejoice over thee with joy; he will rest in his love, he will joy over thee with singing." - Zephaniah 3:17

"According as his divine power hath given unto us all things that pertain unto life and godliness, through the knowledge of him that hath called us to glory and virtue:" - 2 Peter 1:3

"Touching the Almighty, we cannot find him out: he is excellent in power, and in judgment, and in plenty of justice: he will not afflict." - Job 37:23

"Thou therefore, my son, be strong in the grace that is in Christ Jesus." - 2 Timothy 2:1

"And be not conformed to this world: but be ye transformed by the renewing of your mind, that ye may prove what is that good, and acceptable, and perfect, will of God." - Romans 12:2

"Arise; for this matter belongeth unto thee: we also will be with thee: be of good courage, and do it." - Ezra 10:4

"The Lord is good, a strong hold in the day of trouble; and he knoweth them that trust in him." - Nahum 1:7

"For with God nothing shall be impossible." - Luke 1:37

"I can do all things through Christ which strengtheneth me." - Philippians 4:13

"But they that wait upon the Lord shall renew their strength; they shall mount up with wings as eagles; they shall run, and not be weary; and they shall walk, and not faint." - Isaiah 40:31

"Be strong and of a good courage, fear not, nor be afraid of them: for the Lord thy God, he it is that doth go with thee; he will not fail thee, nor forsake thee." - Deuteronomy 31:6

"Fear thou not; for I am with thee: be not dismayed; for I am thy God: I will strengthen thee; yea, I will help thee with the right hand of my righteousness." - Isaiah 41:10

"And he said unto me, My grace is sufficient for thee: for my strength is made perfect in weakness. Most gladly therefore will I rather glory in my infirmities, that the power of Christ may rest upon me. Therefore I take pleasure in infirmities, in reproaches, in necessities, in persecutions, in distresses for Christ's sake: for when I am weak, then am I strong." - 2 Corinthians 12:9-10

"There hath no temptation taken you but such as is common to man: but God is faithful, who will not suffer you to be tempted above that ye are able; but will with the temptation also make a way to escape, that ye may be able to bear it." - 1 Corinthians 10:13

"For the Lord your God is he that goeth with you, to fight for you against your enemies, to save you." - Deuteronomy 20:4

"Be of good courage, and he shall strengthen your heart, all ye that hope in the Lord." - Psalms 31:24

"The Lord is my strength and song, and he is become my salvation: he is my God, and I will prepare him an habitation; my father's God, and I will exalt him." - Exodus 15:2

"Watch ye, stand fast in the faith, quit you like men, be strong." - 1 Corinthians 16:13

"God is our refuge and strength, a very present help in trouble. Therefore will not we fear, though the earth be removed, and though the mountains be carried into the midst of the sea; Though the waters thereof roar and be troubled, though the mountains shake with the swelling thereof. Selah." - Psalm 46:1-3

"The Lord is my light and my salvation; whom shall I fear? the Lord is the strength of my life; of whom shall I be afraid?" - Psalm 27:1

"I know both how to be abased, and I know how to abound: every where and in all things I am instructed both to be full and to be hungry, both to abound and to suffer need. I can do all things through Christ which strengthenth me." - Philippians 4:12-13

"For which cause we faint not; but through our outward man perish, yet inward man is renewed day by day." - 2 Corinthians 4:16

"But be not thou far from me, O Lord: O my strength, haste thee to help me." - Psalm 22:19

"Look unto me, and be ye saved, all the ends of the earth: for I am God, and there is none else. I have sworn by myself, the word is gone out of my mouth in righteousness, and shall not return, That unto me every knee shall bow, every tongue shall swear. Surely, shall one say, in the Lord have I righteousness and strength: even to him shall men come; and all that are incensed against him shall be ashamed." - Isaiah 45:22-25

"My mouth shall shew forth thy righteousness and thy salvation all the day: for I know not the numbers thereof. I will go in the strength of the Lod God: I will make mention of thy righteousness, even of thine only." - Psalm 71:15-16

Eternal Life

Jesus is the resurrection and the life. Whoever believes in Him and accepts Him as their personal Savior, will receive the gift of "eternal life." Eternal life doesn't get started once you die. It starts by faith, as soon as you accept Jesus into your life.

We were created in the image of God and according to the likeness of God, to express the life of God. The moment Adam and Eve ate from the forbidden tree, they became separated from the Life of God and each of us are born, "in Adam." Therefore, being the all-loving and all-compassionate God that He is, came to earth in human form, lived in sin, but lived a sinless life, died on a cross, on Calvary's hill, then rose from the dead, in power over death. Why did He die? For our sins! He was the sacrifice that could only satisfy the wrath of a holy God, against sin. He died as the propitiation, the seat of mercy, because we can't please God in and of ourselves. Jesus covered our sins, with His blood, forever. He died for us, so that we could have life for all eternity. He is the Eternal Life.

"For God so loved the world, that he gave his only begotten Son, that whosoever believeth in him should not perish, but have everlasting life." - John 3:16

"For the wages of sin is death; but the gift of God is eternal life through Jesus Christ our Lord." - Romans 6:23

"And this is life eternal, that they might know thee the only true God, and Jesus Christ, whom thou hast sent." - John 17:3

"And these shall go away into everlasting punishment: but the righteous into life eternal." - Matthew 25:46

"For by grace are ye saved through faith; and that not of yourselves: it is the gift of God." - Ephesians 2:8

"And Jesus said unto him, Verily I say unto thee, To day shalt thou be with me in paradise." - Luke 23:43

"But the fearful, and unbelieving, and the abominable, and murderers, and whoremongers, and sorcerers, and idolaters, and all liars, shall have their part in the lake which burneth with fire and brimstone: which is the second death." - Revelation 21:8

"Whosoever shall call upon the name of the Lord shall be saved." - Romans 10:13

"Be no deceived; God is not mocked: for whatsoever a man soweth, that shall he also reap. For he that soweth to his flesh shall of the flesh reap corruption; but he that soweth to the Spirit shall of the Spirit reap life everlasting." - Galatians 6:7-8

"If we confess our sins, he is faithful and just to forgive us our sins, and to cleanse us from all unrighteousness." - 1 John 1:9

"And I give unto them eternal life; and they shall neither perish, neither shall any man pluck them out of my hand. My Father, which gave them me, is greater than all; and no man is able to pluck them out of my Father's hand. I and my Father are one." - John 10:28-30

"Not every one that saith unto me, Lord, Lord, shall enter into the kingdom of heaven; but he that doeth the will of my Father which is in heaven." - Matthew 7:21

"Verily, verily, I say unto you, He that heareth my word, and believeth on him that sent me, hath everlasting life, and shall not come into condemnation; but is passed from death unto life." - John 5:24

"For whoso findeth me findeth life, and shall obtain favour of the Lord." - Proverbs 8:35

"But the God of all grace, who hath called us unto his eternal glory by Christ Jesus, after that ye have suffered a while, make you perfect, stablish, strengthen, settle you." - 1 Peter 5:10

"And the world passeth away, and the lust thereof: but he that doeth the will of God abideth for ever." - 1 John 2:17

"While we look not at things which are seen, but at the things which are not seen: for the things which are seen are temporal; but the things which are not seen are eternal." - 2 Corinthians 4:18

"These things have I written unto you that believe on the name of the Son of God; that ye may know that ye have eternal life, and that ye may believe on the name of the Son of God." - 1 John 5:13

"For the wages of sin is death; but the gift of God is eternal life through Jesus Christ our Lord." - Romans 6:23

"Search me, O God, and know my heart: try me, and know my thoughts: And see if there be any wicked way in me, and lead me in the way everlasting." - Psalm 139:23-24

"Enter ye in at the strait gate: for wide is the gate, and broad is the way, that leadeth to destruction, and many there be which go in thereat: Because strait is the gate, and narrow is the way, which leadeth unto life, and few there be that find it." - Matthew 7:13-14

"Fight the good fight of faith, lay hold on eternal life, whereunto thou art also called, and hast professed a good profession before many witnesses." - 1 Timothy 6:12

"But whosoever drinketh of the water that I shall give him shall never thirst; but the water that I shall give him shall be in him a well of water springing up into everlasting life." - John 4:14

"He that findeth his life shall lose it: and he that loseth his life for my sake shall find it." - Matthew 10:39

"Howbeit for this cause I obtained mercy, that in me first Jesus Christ might shew forth all longsuffering, for a pattern to them which should hereafter believe on him to life everlasting." - 1 Timothy 1:16

"For the Lord loveth judgment, and forsaketh not his saints; they are preserved for ever: but the seed of the wicked shall be cut off." - Psalm 37:28

"Wherefore he is able also to save them to the uttermost that come unto God by him, seeing he ever liveth to make intercession for them." - Hebrews 7:25

"Labour not for the meat which perisheth, but for that meat which endureth unto everlasting life, which the Son of man shall give unto you: for him hath God the Father sealed." - John 6:27

"For I have no pleasure in the death of him that dieth, saith the Lord GOD: wherefore turn yourselves, and live ye." - Ezekiel 18:32

"He that keepeth the commandment keepeth his own soul; but he that despiseth his ways shall die." - Proverbs 19:16

"And I heard a great voice out of heaven saying, Behold, the tabernacle of God is with men, and he will dwell with them, and they shall be his people, and God himself shall be with them, and be their God. And God shall wipe away all tears from their eyes; and there shall be no more death, neither sorrow, nor crying, neither shall there be any more pain: for the former things are passed away." - Revelation 21:3-4

Righteous And Righteousness

Righteous is defined as acting in accord with divine or moral law and being free from guilt or sin. Righteousness is defined as a behavior that is morally justifiable or right. Righteousness is one of the attributes of God.

God the Father is righteous and Jesus Christ is His Son and is the Righteous One. True righteousness can never be achieved by living according to Biblical ethics, doing right versus doing wrong. Living righteously can never be accomplished humanly, no matter how hard you try. There is only One who ever has lived right, the Righteous One who is Jesus Christ. That is why He came down from heaven and shed His blood and died upon the cross. Jesus who never sinned, He willingly gave up His life by becoming sin for us. Jesus took our place and became us upon the cross. Jesus became what we were, sin, so that we might become what He is, righteous. Jesus has made unto us righteousness. So we are the righteousness of God in union with Christ, who is life.

"The righteous also shall hold on his way, and he that hath clean hands shall be stronger and stronger." - Job 17:9

"Blessed is the man that walketh not in the counsel of the ungodly, nor standeth in the way of sinners, not sitteth in the seat of the scornful." - Psalm 1:3

"Drop down, ye heavens, from above, and let the skies pour down righteousness: let the earth open, and let them bring forth salvation, and let righteousness spring up together; I the Lord have created it." - Isaiah 45:8

"The righteous perisheth, and no man layeth it to hear: and merciful men are taken away, none considering that the righteous is taken away from evil to come." - Isaiah 57:1-2

"The name of the Lord is a strong tower; the righteous runneth into it, and is safe." - Proverb 18:10

"The heart of the righteous studieth to answer: but the mouth of the wicked poureth out evil things. The Lord is far from the wicked: but he heareth the prayer of the righteous." - Proverbs 15:28-29

"Praise ye the Lord. Blessed is the man that feareth the Lord, that delighteth greatly in his commandments. His seed shall be mighty upon earth: the generation of the upright shall be blessed. Wealth and riches shall be in his house: and his righteousness endureth for ever." - Psalm 112:1-3

"Ye that love the Lord, hate evil: he preserveth the souls of his saints; he delivereth them out of the hand of the wicked. Light is sown for the righteous, and gladness for the upright in heart." - Psalm 97:10-11

"My mouth shall shew forth thy righteousness and thy salvation all the day: for I know not the numbers thereof. I will go in the strength of the Lord God: I will make mention of thy righteousness, even of thine only." - Psalm 71:15-16

"Look unto me, and be ye saved, all the ends of the earth: for I am God, and there is none else. I have sworn by myself, the word is gone out of my mouth in righteousness, and shall not return, That unto me every knee shall bow, every tongue shall swear. Surely, shall one say, in the Lord have I righteousness and strength: even to him shall men come; and all that are incensed against him shall be ashamed." - Isaiah 45:22-25

"Lead me, O Lord, in thy righteousness because of mine enemies; make thy way straight before my face." - Psalm 5:8

"So that a man shall say, Verily there is a reward for the righteous: verily he is a God that judgeth in the earth." - Psalm 58:11

"And they that be wise shall shine as the brightness of the firmament; and they that turn many to righteousness as the stars for ever and ever." - Daniel 12:3

"Then shall the righteous shine forth as the sun in the kingdom of their Father. Who hath ears to hear, let him hear." - Matthew 13:43

"And these shall go away into everlasting punishment: but the righteous into life eternal." - Matthew 25:46

"For ir by one man's offence death reigned by one; much more they which receive abundance of grace and of the gift of righteousness shall reign in life by one, Jesus Christ." - Romans 5:17

"Blessed are they which are persecuted for righteousness' sake: for their's is the kingdom of heaven." - Matthew 5:10

"Blessed are they which do hunger and thirst after righteousness: for they shall be filled." - Matthew 5:6

"I have fought a good fight, I have finished my course, I have kept the faith: Henceforth there is laid up for me a crown of righteousness, which the Lord, the righteous judge, shall give me at that day: and not to me only, but unto all them also that love his appearing." - 2 Timothy 4:7-8

"He that followeth after righteousness and mercy findeth life, righteousness, and honour." - Proverbs 21:21

"Cast thy burden upon the Lord, and he shall sustain thee: he shall never suffer the righteous to be moved." - Psalm 55:22

"But the salvation of the righeous is of the Lord: he is their strength in the time of trouble. And the Lord shall help them, and deliver them: he shall deliver them from the wicked, and save them, because they trust in him." - Psalm 37:39-40

"For the grace of God that bringeth salvation hath appeared to all men, Teaching us that denying ungodliness and worldly lusts, we should live soberly, righteously, and godly, in this present world: Looking for that blessed hope and the glorious appearing of the great God and our Saviour Jesus Christ. Who gave himself for us, that he might redeem us from all iniquity, and purify unto himself a peculiar people, zealous of good works." - Titus 2:11-14

"But seek ye first the kingdom of God, and his righteousness; and all these things shall be added unto you." - Matthew 6:33

"Sow to yourselves in righteousness, reap in mercy; break up your fallow ground: for it is time to seek the Lord, till he come and rain righteousness upon you." - Hosea 10:12

"For thou, Lord, wilt bless the righteous; with favour wilt thou compass him as with a shield." - Psalm 5:12

"The steps of a good man are ordered by the Lord: and he delighteth in his way. Though he fall, he shall not be utterly cast down: for the Lord upholdeth him with his hand." - Psalm 37:23-24

"The righteous shall inherit the land, and dwell therein for ever. The mouth of the righteous speaketh wisdom, and his tongue talketh of judgment. The law of his God is in his heart; none of his steps shall slide. The wicked watcheth the righteous and seeketh to slay him." - Psalm 37:29-32

"But and if ye suffer for righteousness' sake, happy are ye: and be not afraid of their terror, neither be troubled." - 1 Peter 3:13

"Finally, brethren, whatsoever things are true, whatsoever things are just, whatsoever things are lovely, whatsoever things are of good report; if there be any virtue, and if there be any praise, think on these things." - Philippians 4:8

"And let us not be weary in well doing: for in due season we shall reap, if we faint not." - Galatians 6:9

"In righteousness shalt thou be established; thou shalt be far from oppression; for thou shalt not fear: and from terror; for it shall not come near thee." - Isaiah 54:14

"Treasures of wickedness profit nothing: but righteousness delivereth from death. The Lord will not suffer the soul of the righteous to famish: but he casteth away the substance of the wicked." - Proverbs 10:2-3

"Lord, who shall abide in thy tabernacle? who shall dwell in thy holy hill? He that walketh uprightly, and worketh righteousness, and speakeith the truth in his heart." - Psalm 15:1-2

"For the eyes of the Lord are over the righteous, and his ears are open unto their prayers: but the face of the Lord is against them that do evil." - 1 Peter 3:12

"And the fruit of righteousness is sown in peace of them that make peace." - James 3:18

"The wicked worketh a deceitful work: but to him that soweth righteousness shall be a sure reward. As righteousness tendeth to life: so he that pursueth evil pursueth it to his own death." - Proverbs 11:18-19

"Not by works of righteousness which we have done, but according to his mercy he saved us, by the washing of regeneration, and renewing of the Holy Ghost." - Titus 3:5

Provision

God promised to supply ALL of our needs. God is our Provider. He is our Source. He is our infinite Supplier who never or could never ever run out of anything and He never run short of anything.

God desires to meet every single one of our needs, throughout our entire life. Jesus said, "Your heavenly Father knows what you need before you ask him."

Whatever your needs are and all the needs of your life, God knows all about them and He is able to supply and meet all of your needs.

God is all-powerful, all-compassionate, all-wise, all-loving, all-comforting, and so much more. He is the God that supplies it ALL. After all, one of God's names is JEHOVAH JIREH, which means "The Lord Will Provide."

"But my God shall supply all your need according to his riches in glory by Christ Jesus." - Philippians 4:19

"But if any provide not for his own, and specially for those of his own house, he hath denied the faith, and is worse than an infidel."
- 1 Timothy 5:8

"And God is able to make all grace abound toward you; that ye always having all sufficiency in all things, may abound to every good work:" - 2 Corinthians 9:8

"Therefore take no thought, saying, What shall we eat? or, What shall we drink? or, Wherewihal shall we be clothed? (For after all these things do the Gentiles seek:) for your heavenly Father knoweth that ye have need of all these things. But seek ye first the kingdom of God, and his righteousness; and all these things shall be added unto you." - Matthew 6:31-33

"The Lord is my shepherd; I shall not want." - Psalm 23:1

"Who provideth for the raven his food? when his young ones cry unto God, they wander for lack of meat." - Job 38:41

"Every moving thing that liveth shall be meat for you; even as the green herb have I given you all things." - Genesis9:3

"For I know the thoughts that I think toward you, saith the Lord, thoughts of peace, and not of evil, to give you an expected end."
- Jeremiah 29:11

"I have been young, and now am old; yet have I not seen the righteous forsaken, nor his seed begging bread." - Psalm 37:25

"If ye then, being evil, know how to give good gifts unto your children, how much more shall your Father which is in heaven give good things to them that ask him?" - Matthew 7:11

"The young lions do lack, and suffer hunger: but they that seek the Lord shall not want any good thing." - Psalm 34:10

"Consider the ravens: for they neither sow nor reap; which neither have storehouse nor barn; and God feedeth them: how much more are ye better than the fowls?" - Luke 12:24

"Let your conversation be without covetousness; and be content with such things as ye have: for he hath said, I will never leave thee nor forsake thee." - Hebrews 13:5

"Be careful for nothing; but in every thing by prayer and supplication with thanksgiving let your requests be made known unto God." - Philippians 4:6

"According as his divine power hath given unto us all things that pertain unto life and godliness, through the knowledge of him that hath called us to glory and virtue:" - 2 Peter 1:3

"He that spared not his own Son, but delivered him up for us all, how shall he not with him also freely give us all things?" - Romans 8:32

"The thief cometh not, but for to steal, and to kill, and to destroy: I am come that they might have life, and that they might have it more abundantly." - John 10:10

"But even the very hairs of your head are all numbered. Fear not therefore: ye are of more value than many sparrows." - Luke 12:7

"Therefore I say unto you, Take no thought for your life, what ye shall eat, or what ye shall drink; nor yet for your body, what ye shall put on. Is not the life more than meat, and the body than raiment? Behold the fowls of the air: for they sow not, neither do they reap, nor gather into barns; yet your heavenly Father feedeth them. Are ye not much better than they?" - Matthew 6:25-26

"I will abundantly bless her poor with vision: I will satisfy her poor with bread." - Psalm 132:15

"And it shall come to pass, if thou shalt hearken diligently unto the voice of the Lord thy God, to observe and to do all his commandments which I command thee this day, that the Lord thy God will set thee on high above all nations of the earth:" - Deuteronomy 28:1

"Bring ye all the tithes into the storehouse, that there may be meat in mine house, and prove me now herewith, saith the Lord of hosts, if I will not open you the windows of heaven, and pour you out a blessing, that there shall not be room enough to receive it." - Malachi 3:10

"That I will give you the rain of your land in his due season, the first rain and the latter rain, that thou mayest gather in thy corn, and thy wine, and thine oil." - Deuteronomy 11:14

"Give, and it shall be given unto you; good measure, pressed down, and shaken together, and running over, shall men give into your bosom. For with the same measure that ye mete withal it shall be measured to you again." - Luke 6"38

"(As it is written, He hath dispersed abroad; he hath given to the poor: his righteousness remaineth for ever. Now he that ministereth seed to the sower both minister bread for your food, and multiply your seed sown, and increase the fruits of your righteousness;)" - 2 Corinthians 9:8-10

"Beloved, I wish above all things that thou mayest prosper and be in health, even as thy soul prospereth." - 3 John 1:2

"He hath given meat unto them that fear him: he will ever be mindful of his covenant." - Psalm 111:5

"Honour the Lord with thy substance, and with the firstfruits of all thine increase: So shall thy barns be filled with plenty, and thy presses shall burst out with new wine." - Proverbs 3:9-10

"Ask, and it shall be given you; seek, and ye shall find; knock, and it shall be opened unto you: For every one that asketh receiveth; and he that seeketh findeth; and to him that knocketh it shall be opened." - Matthew 7:7-8

"Come unto me, all ye that labour and are heavy laden, and I will give you rest." - Matthew 11:28

"Not that I speak in respect of want: for I have learned, in whatsoever state I am, therewith to be content." - Philippians 4:11

"If any of you lack wisdom, let him ask of God, that giveth to all men liberally, and upbraideth not; and it shall be given him." - James 1:5

"The Lord is my shepherd; I shall not want. He maketh me to lie down in green pastures: he leadeth me beside the still waters. He restoreth my soul: he leadeth me in the paths of righteousness for his name's sake. Yea, though I walk through the valley of the shadow of death, I will fear no evil: for thou art with me: thy rod and thy staff they comfort me. Thou preparest a table before me in the presence of mine enemies: thou anointest my head with oil; my cup runneth over. Surely goodness and mercy shall follow me all the days of my life: and I will dwell in the house of the Lord for ever." - Psalm 23:1-6

"The blessing of the Lord, it maketh rich, and he addeth no sorrow with it." - Proverbs 10:22

"And in that day ye shall ask me nothing. Verily, verily, I say unto you, Whatsoever ye shall ask the Father in my name, he will give it you." - John 16:23

"Let us therefore come boldly unto the throne of grace, that we may obtain mercy, and find grace to help in time of need." - Hebrews 4:16

"If ye abide in me, and my words abide in you, ye shall ask what ye will, and it shall be done unto you." - John 15:7

"For let not that man think that he shall receive any thing of the Lord." - James 1:7

Trust

Trust is the confidence in the honesty or integrity of a person or thing. A firm belief in the integrity, ability or character. When it comes to God, TRUST = BELIEVE.

Trusting in God, is believing in the promises of God in all circumstances, although you don't understand it and the evidence says, "it can't happen." The Bible clearly tells us to trust in the Lord with all your heart and lean not on your own understanding.

God wants us to just trust Him. God has proven, time and time again, that He can be trusted. You must trust in the Lord with ALL your heart. Not some of it, but ALL of it. You will face some very trying times in life. Who are you going to trust completely? In every aspect of your life, God wants you to be confident in Him, and rely completely upon Him. God desires for you to come to a place of total surrender. He wants you to allow Him to rule supremely in your life. Don't trust yourself. Don't lean to your own understanding. Put your trust in God, not your world experiences. Put your trust in God's Word. Trust Him completely and totally.

"He that dwelleth in the secret place of the most High shall abide under the shadow of the Almighty. I will say of the Lord, He is my refuge and my fortress: my God; in him will I trust." - Psalm 91:1-2

"For we walk by faith, not by sight." - 2 Corinthians 5:7

"Trust in the Lord, and do good; so shalt thou dwell in the land, and verily thou shalt be fed." Psalm 37:3

"And we have known and believed the love that God hath to us. God is love; and he that dwelleth in love dwelleth in God, and God in him." - 1 John 4:16

In God is my salvation and my glory: the rock of my strength, and my refuge, is in God." - Psalm 62:7

"When thou passest through the waters, I will be with thee; and through the rivers, they shall not overflow thee: when thou walkest through the fire, thou shalt not be burned; neither shall the flame kindle upon thee." - Isaiah 43:2

"The God of my rock; in him will I trust: he is my shield, and the horn of my salvation, my high tower, and my refuge, my saviour; thou savest me from violence." - 2 Samuel 22:3

He will not suffer thy foot to be moved: he that keepeth thee will not slumber." - Psalm 121:13

"Behold the fowls of the air: for they sow not, neither do they reap, nor gather into barns; yet your heavenly Father feedeth them. Are ye not much better than they?" - Matthew 6:26

"So that we may boldly say, The Lord is my helper, and I will not fear what man shall do unto me." - Hebrews 13:6

"Wait on the Lord; be of good courage, and he shall strengthen thine heart: wait, I say, on the Lord." - Psalm 27:14

"Trust in the Lord with all thine heart; and lean not unto thine own understanding. In all thy ways acknowledge him, and he shall direct thy paths." - Proverbs 3:5-6

"The fear of man bringeth a snare: but whoso putteth his trust in the Lord shall be safe." - Proverbs 29:25

"Whom have I in heaven but thee? and there is none upon earth that I desire beside thee." - Psalm 73:25

"He that handleth a matter wisely shall find good: and whoso trusteth in the Lord, happy is he." - Proverbs 16:20

"Oh how great is thy goodness, which thou hast laid up for them that fear thee; which thou hast wrought for them that trust in thee before the sons of men!" - Psalm 31:19

"The Lord is good, a strong hold in the day of trouble; and he knoweth them that trust in him." - Hahum 1:7

"Commit thy way unto the Lord; trust also in him; and he shall bring it to pass. And he shall bring forth thy righteousness as the light, and thy judgment as the noonday." - Psalm 37:5-6

"Blessed is the man that trusteth in the Lord, and whose hope the Lord is. For he shall be as a tree planted by the waters, and that spreadeth out her roots by the river, and shall not see when heat cometh, but her leaf shall be green; and shall not be careful in the year of drought, neither shall cease from yielding fruit." - Jeremiah 17:7-8

"In God I will praise his word, in God I have put my trust; I will not fear what flesh can do unto me." - Psalm 56:4

"The Lord is nigh unto all them that call upon him, to all that call upon him in truth." - Psalm 145:18

"And if we know that he hear us, whatsoever we ask, we know that we have the petitions that we desired of him." - 1 John 5:15

"Preserve me, O God: for in thee do I put my trust." - Psalm 16:1

"Let not your heart be troubled: ye believe in God, believe also in me." - John 14:1

"It is better to trust in the Lord than to put confidence in man." - Psalm 118:8

"Thou wilt keep him in perfect peace, whose mind is stayed on thee: because he trusteth in thee." - Isaiah 26:3

"The Lord is my strength and my shield; my heart trusted in him, and I am helped: therefore my heart greatly rejoiceth; and with my song will I praise him." - Psalm 28:7

"And Jesus said unto them, Because of your unbelief: for verily I say unto you, If ye have faith as a grain of mustard seed, ye shall say unto this mountain, Remove hence to yonder place; and it shall remove; and nothing shall be impossible unto you." - Matthew 17:20

"And they that know thy name will put their trust in thee: for thou, Lord, hast not forsaken them that seek thee." - Psalm 9:10

"But I have trusted in thy mercy; my heart shall rejoice in thy salvation. I will sing unto the Lord, because he hath dealt bountifully with me." - Psalm 13:5-6

"I had fainted, unless I had believed to see the goodness of the Lord in the land of the living." - Psalm 27:3

"Though an host should encamp against me, my heart shall not fear: though war should rise against me, in this will I be confident." - Psalm 27:3

"Trust in him at all time; ye people, pour out your heart before him: God is a refuge for us. Selah." - Psalm 62:8

His Plans For US

God has some amazing plans for you. God created you for a unique and special purpose, and He has equipped you with a special gift for your unique and special purpose.

God has a perfect plan for your life. A plan that will bring Him honor and glory. He knows your future and His plans are good and full of hope. Does this mean you will not endure any kind of pain or suffering? Absolutely not! God never promised us that, but He did tell us that He would never leave us nor forsake us.

God has a plan for your life. He loves you. He wants to have a relationship with you. He wants you to return the love. Isn't it just wonderful that God has plans for your life!

"For I know the thoughts that I think toward you, saith the Lord, thoughts of peace, and not of evil, to give you an expected end."
- Jeremiah 29:11

"Trust in the Lord with all thine heart; and lean not unto thine own understanding. In all thy ways acknowledge him, and he shall direct thy paths." - Proverbs 3:5-6

"To every thing there is a season, and a time to every under the heaven: A time to be born, and a time to die; a time to plant, and a time to pluck up that which is planted; A time to kill, and a time to heal; a time to break down, and a time to build up; A time to weep, and a time to laugh; a time to mourn, and a time to dance; A time to cast away stones, and a time to gather stones together; a time to embrace, and a time to refrain from embracing; A time to get, and a time to lose; a time to keep, and a time to cast away; A time to rend, and a time to sew; a time to keep silence, and a time to speak; A time to love, and a time to hate; a time of war, and a time of peace." - Ecclesiastes 3:1-8

"A man's heart deviseth his way: but the Lord directeth his steps." - Proverbs 16:9

"And the Lord shall guide thee continually, and satisfy thy soul in drought, and make fat thy bones: and thou shalt be like a watered garden, and like a spring of water, whose waters fail not." - Isaiah 58:11

"Before I formed thee in the belly I knew thee; and before thou camest forth out of the womb I sanctified thee, and I ordained thee a prophet unto the nations." - Jeremiah 1:5

"If ye abide in me, and my words abide in you, ye shall ask what ye will, and it shall be done unto you." - John 15:7

"The steps of a good man are ordered by the Lord: and he delighteth in his way." - Psalm 37:23

"Trust in the Lord with all thine heart; and lean not unto thine own understanding." - Proverbs 3:5

"But as it is written, Eye hath not seen, nor ear heard, neither have entered into the heart of man, the things which God hath prepared for them that love him." - 1 Corinthians 2:9

"And be not conformed to this world: but be ye transformed by the renewing of your mind, that ye may prove what is that good, and acceptable, and perfect, will of God." - Romans 12:2

"Wait on the Lord: be of good courage, and he shall strengthen thine heart: wait, I say, on the Lord." - Psalm 27:4

"But they that wait upon the Lord shall renew their strength; they shall mount up with wings as eagles; they shall run, and not be weary; and they shall walk, and not faint." - Isaiah 40:31

"I will instruct thee and teach thee in the way which thou shalt go: I will guide thee with mine eye." - Psalm 32:8

"For surely there is an end; and thine expectation shall not be cut off." - Proverbs 23:18

"For we are his workmanship, created in Christ Jesus unto good works, which God hath before ordained that we should walk in them." - Ephesians 2:10

"The Lord is not slack concerning his promise, as some men count slackness; but is longsuffering to us-ward, not willing that any should perish, but that all should come to repentance." - 2 Peter 3:9

"Now unto him that is able to do exceeding abundantly above all that we ask or think, according to the power that worketh in us." - Ephesians 3:20

"For God so loved the world, that he gave his only begotten Son, that whosoever believeth in him should not perish, but have everlasting life." - John 3:16

"Rejoice evermore. Pray without ceasing. In every thing give thanks: for this is the will of God in Christ Jesus concerning you." - 1 Thessalonians 5:16-18

"The Lord of hosts hath sworn, saying, Surely as I have thought, so shall it come to pass; and as I have purposed, so shall it stand." - Isaiah 14:24

"Delight thyself also in the Lord; and he shall give thee the desires of thine heart." - Psalm 37:4

"Thy word is a lamp unto my feet, and a light unto my path. I have sworn, and I will perform it, that I will keep thy righteous judgments." - Psalm 119: 105-106

"Being confident of this very thing, that he which hath begun a good work in you will perform it until the day of Jesus Christ." - Philippians 1:6

"Be strong and of a good courage, fear not, nor be afraid of them: for the Lord thy God, he it is that doth go with thee; he will not fail thee, nor forsake thee." - Deuteronomy 31:6

"The Lord will perfect that which concerneth me: thy mercy, O Lord, endureth for ever: forsake not the works of thine own hands." - Psalm 138:8

"For my thoughts are not your thoughts, neither are your ways my ways, saith the Lord. For as the heavens are higher than the earth, so are my ways higher than your ways, and my thoughts than your thoughts." - Isaiah 55:8-9

"If ye love me, keep my commandments." - John 14:15

"So then faith cometh by hearing, and hearing by the word of God." - Romans 10:17

"I know that thou canst do every thing and that no thought can be withholden from thee." - Job 42:2

"For the vision is yet for an appointed time, but at the end it shall speak, and not lie: though it tarry, wait for it; because it will surely come, it will not tarry." - Habakkuk 2:3

"When thou passest through the waters, I will be with thee; and through the rivers, they shall not overflow thee: when thou walkest through the fire, thou shalt not be burned: neither shall the flame kindle upon thee." - Isaiah 43:2

"To every thing there is a season, and a time to every purpose under the heaven:" - Ecclesiastes 3:1

"Who will have all men to be saved, and to come unto the knowledge of the truth." - 1 Timothy 2:4

"There hath no temptation taken you but such as is common to man: but God is faithful, who will not suffer you to be tempted above that ye are able; but will with the temptation also make a way to escape, that ye may be able to bear it." - 1 Corinthians 10:13

"Who hath saved us, and called us with an holy calling, not according to our works, but according to his own purpose and grace, which was given us in Christ Jesus before the world began." - 2 Timothy 1:9

"Many, O Lord my God, are thy wonderful works which thou hast done, and thy thoughts which are to us-ward: they cannot be reckoned up in order unto thee: if I would declare and speak of them, they are more than can be numbered." - Psalm 40:5

"Declaring the end from the beginning, and from ancient times the things that are not yet done, saying, My counsel shall stand, and I will do all my pleasure:" - Isaiah 46:10

"Thou tellest my wanderings put thou my tears into thy bottle: are they not in thy books?" - Psalm 56:8

"Jesus answered and said unto him, If a man love me, he will keep my words; and my Father will love him, and we will come unto him, and make our abode with him. He that loveth me not keepeth not my saying: and the word which ye hear is not mine, but the Father's which sent me." - John 14:23-24

"Ask, and it shall be given you; seek, and ye shall find; knock, and it shall be opened unto you: For every one that asketh receiveth; ad he that seeketh findeth; and to him that knocketh it shall be opened." - Matthew 7:7-8

"In whom also we have obtained an inheritance, being predestinated according to the purpose of him who worketh all things after the counsel of his own will." - Ephesians 1:11

"For the wages of sin is death; but the gift of God is eternal life through Jesus Christ our Lord." - Romans 6:23

"Seek the Lord and his strength, seek his face continually, Remember his marvellous works that he hath done, his wonders and the judgments of his mouth;" - 1 Chronicles 16:11-12

"For this God is our God for ever and ever: he will be our guide even unto death." - Psalm 48:14

"According as he hath chosen us in him before the foundation of the world, that we should be holy and without blame before him in love. Having predestinated us unto the adoption of children by Jesus Christ to himself according to the good pleasure of his will." - Ephesians 1:4-5

"But the Comforter, which is the Holy Ghost, whom the Father will send in my name, he shall teach you all things, and bring all things to your remembrance, whatsoever I have said unto you." - John 14:26

"And we know that all things work together for good to them that love God, to them who are the called according to his purpose. For whom he did foreknow, he also did predestinate to be conformed to the image of his Son, that he might be the firstborn among many brethren." - Romans 8:28-29

"I can do all things through Christ which strengtheneth me." - Philippians 4:13

"For by grace are ye saved through faith; and that not of yourselves: it is the gift of God; Not of works, lest any man should boast." - Ephesians 2:8-9

"This is the purpose that is purposed upon the whole earth: and this is the hand that is stretched out upon all the nations. For the Lord of hosts hath purposed, and who shall disannul it? and his hand is stretched out, and who shall turn it back?" - Isaiah 14:26-27

"Commit thy works unto the Lord, and thy thoughts shall be established." - Proverbs 16:3

"Wherein God, willing more abundantly to shew unto the heirs of promise the immutability of his counsel, confirmed it by an oath:" - Hebrews 6:17

"Give, and it shall be given unto you; good measure, pressed down, and shaken together, and running over, shall men give into your bosom. For with the same measure that ye mete withal it shall be measured to you again." - Luke 6:38

"For now we see through a glass darkly; but then face to face: now I know in part; but then shall I know even as also I am known." - 1 Corinthians 13:12

"But my God shall supply all your need according to his riches in glory by Christ Jesus." - Philippians 4:19

"For we know in part, and we prophesy in part." - 1 Corinthians 13:9

"Be not carried about with divers and strange doctrines. For it is a good thing that the heart be established with grace; not with meats, which have not profited them that have been occupied therein." - Hebrews 13:9

"Now the God of peace, that brought again from the dead our Lord Jesus, that great shepherd of the sheep, through the blood of the everlasting covenant, Make you perfect in every good work to do his will, working in you that which is wellpleasing in his sight, through Jesus Christ; to whom be glory for ever and ever. Amen." - Hebrews 13:20-21

Healing Physical, Emotional, And Spiritually

God is an excellent Physican. God is a Healer! God is known by many names in the Bible. Jehovah-Rapha is one such name and it means, "God who heals." God's very nature is healing and God wants to provide healing to His children.

We live in a world that is full of darkness, hurt, pain, suffering, whether physical, spiritual, or emotional. Physical pain, like cancer or arthritis. Spiritual pain, like being separated from God. Emotional pain, like the loss of a loved one, divorce, or a job.

It is through the redemption of Jesus that through God there is healing, for our every aspect, body, mind, and soul. The Bible reminds us of this healing through Jesus. "By his wounds you have been healed." Healed from what? Our sins! It is our sins that separates us from God. Our physical healing and our emotional healing.

Whatever pain you may be suffering, because the Lord really loves you, He desires to fix your broken wounded heart, heal your body, and mend your relationship.

"He healeth the broken in heart, and bindeth up their wounds." - Psalm 147:3

"The Lord will strengthen him upon the bed of languishing: thou wilt make all his bed in his sickness." - Psalm 41:3

"Heal me, O Lord, and I shall be healed; save me, and I shall be saved: for thou art my praise." - Jeremiah 17:14

"For I will restore health unto thee, and I will heal thee of thy wounds, saith the Lord; because they called thee an Outcast, saying, This is Zion, whom no man seeketh after." - Jeremiah 30:17

"My son, attend to my words; incline thine ear unto my sayings, Let them not depart from thine eyes; keep them in the midst of thine heart. For they are life unto those that find them, and health to all their flesh." - Proverbs 4:20-22

"Then they cry unto the Lord in their trouble, and he saveth them out of their distresses. He sent his word, and healed them, and delivered them from their destruction." - Psalm 107:19-20

"And ye shall serve the Lord your God, and he shall bless thy bread, and thy water; and I will take sickness away from the midst of thee." - Exodus 23:25

"Then shall thy light break forth as the morning, and thine health shall spring forth speedily: and thy righteousness shall go before thee; the glory of the Lord shall be thy rereward." - Isaiah 58:8

"And he said unto her, Daughter, thy faith hath made thee whole; go in peace, and be whole of thy plague." - Mark 5:34

"But when Jesus heard it, he answered him saying, Fear not: believe only, and she shall be made whole." - Luke 8:50

"Is any sick among you? let him call for the elders of the church; and let them pray over him, anointing him with oil in the name of the Lord: And the prayer of faith shall save the sick, and the Lord shall raise him up; and if he have committed sins, they shall be forgiven him." - James 5:14-15

"O Lord my God, I cried unto thee, and thou hast healed me." - Psalm 30:2

"Fear thou not; for I am with thee: be not dismayed; for I am thy God: I will strengthen thee; yea, I will help thee; yea, I will uphold thee with the right hand of my righteousness." - Isaiah 41:10

"Behold, I will bring it health and cure, and I will cure them, and will reveal unto them the abundance of peace and truth." - Jeremiah 33:6

"Bless the Lord, O my soul, and forget not all his benefits: Who forgiveth all thine iniquities; who healeth all thy diseases." - Psalm 103:2-3

"Confess your faults one to another, and pray one for another, that ye may be healed. The effectual ferent prayer of a righteous man availeth much." - James 5:16

"Who his own self bare our sins in his own body on the tree, that we, being dead to sins, should live unto righteousness: by whose stripes ye were healed." - 1 Peter 2:24

"The righteous cry, and the Lord heareth, and delivereth them out of all their troubles. The Lord is nigh unto them that are of a broken heart; and saveth such as be of a contrite spirit. Many are the afflictions of the righteous: but the Lord delivereth him out of them all. He keepeth all his bones: not one of them is broken. Evil shall slay the wicked: and they that hate the righteous shall be desolate. The Lord redeemeth the soul of his servants: and none of them that trust in him shall be desolate." - Psalm 34:17-22

"Beloved, I wish above all things that thou mayest prosper and be in health, even as thy soul prospereth." - 3 John 1:2

"I have seen his ways, and will heal him: I will lead him also, and restore comforts unto him and to his mourners. I create the fruit of the lips; Peace, peace to him that is near, saith the Lord; and I will heal him." - Isaiah 57:18-19

"And God shall wipe away all tears from their eyes; and there shall be no more death, neither sorrow, nor crying, neither shall there be any more pain: for the former things are passed away." - Revelation 21:4

"The Lord is my shepherd; I shall not want. He maketh me to lie down in green pastures: he leadeth me beside the still waters. He restoreth my soul: he leadeth me in the paths of righteousness for his name's sake. Yea, though I walk through the valley of the shadow of death, I will fear no evil: for thou art with me; thy rod and thy staff they comfort me. Thou preparest a table before me in the presence of mine enemies: thou anoinest my head with oil; my cup runneth over. Surely goodness and mercy shall follow me all the days of my life: and I will dwell in the house of the Lord for ever." - Psalm 23

"Trust in the Lord with all thine heart; and lean not unto thine own understanding. In all thy ways acknowledge him, and he shall direct thy paths. Be not wise in thine own eyes: fear the Lord, and depart from evil. It shall be health to thy navel, and marrow to thy bones." - Proverbs 3:5-8

"Pleasant words are as an honeycomb, sweet to the soul, and health to the bones." - Proverbs 16:24

"A merry heart doeth good like a medicine; but a broken spirit drieth the bones." - Proverbs 17:22

"Surely he hath borne our griefs, and carried our sorrows: yet we did esteem him stricken, smitten of God, and afflicted. But he was wounded for our transgressions, he was bruised for our iniquities: the chastisement of our peace was upon him; and with his stripes we are healed." - Isaiah 53:4-5

"And said, If thou wilt diligently hearken to the voice of the Lord thy God, and wilt do that which is right in his sight, and wilt give ear to his commandments, and keep all his statues, I will put none of these diseases upon thee, which I have brought upon the Egyptians: for I am the Lord that healeth thee." - Exodus 15:26

"By stretching forth thine hand to heal; and that signs and wonders may be done by the name of thy holy child Jesus." - Acts 4:30

"No weapon that is formed against thee shall prosper; and every tongue that shall rise against thee in judgment thou shalt condemn. This is the heritage of the servants of the Lord, and their righteousness is of me, saith the Lord." - Isaiah 54:17

"But unto you that fear my name shall the Sun of righteousness arise with healing in his wings; and ye shall go forth, and grow up as calves of the stall." - Malachi 4:2

"Take my yoke, upon you,and learn of me; for I am meek and lowly in heart: and ye shall find rest unto your souls. For my yoke is easy, and my burden is light." - Matthew 11:28-29

"Be careful for nothing; but in every thing by prayer and supplication with thanksgiving let your requests be made known unto God." - Philippians 4:6

Salvation

What is Salvation? Salvation is the deliverance from danger or suffering. Biblically, Salvation is the deliverance and saving from sin and its consequences. Salvation is not only being saved from something, but also being save to someone.

When we accept Jesus Christ as our personal Savior, then Jesus comes into our lives and covers our sin. How? By His precious Blood. Through the Blood that was shed for us. You can't get saved by any other way. You can't get saved by any kind of ceremony and no other way, nor system, no matter how sacred you may think it to be. Salvation can only come through our Lord Jesus Christ, through the blood that was shed for us.

Salvation is not in works or rituals or obedience to rules. Salvation comes when you believe in the Lord Jesus Christ and His death on the cross. The Bible clearly says that all who calls upon the name of the Lord shall be saved.

"For with the heart man believeth unto righteousness; and with the mouth confession is made unto salvation." - Romans 10:10

"And they said, Believe on the Lord Jesus Christ, and thou shalt be saved, and thy house." - Acts 16:31

"Neither is there salvation in any other: for there is none other name under heaven given among men, whereby we must be saved." - Acts 4:12

"Who hath saved us, and called us with an holy calling, not according to our works, but according to his own purpose and grace, which was given us in Christ Jesus before the world began." - 2 Timothy 1:9

"Truly my soul waiteth upon God: from him cometh my salvation." - Psalm 62:1

"And it shall come to pass, that whosoever shall call on the name of the Lord shall be saved." - Acts 2:21

"For the grace of God that bringeth salvation hath appeared to all men, Teaching us that, denying ungodliness and worldly lusts, we should live soberly, righteously, and godly, in this present world." - Titus 2:11-12

"For the Son of man is come to seek and to save that which was lost." - Luke 19-10

"So Christ was once offered to bear the sins of many; and unto them that look for him shall he appear the second time without sin unto salvation." - Hebrews 9:28

"The Lord is not slack concerning his promise, as some men count slackness; but is longsuffering to us-ward, not willing that any should perish, but that all should come to repentance." - 2 Peter 3:9

"He that believeth and is baptized shall be saved; but he that believeth not shall be damned." - Mark 16:16

"For scarcely for a righteous man will one die: yet peradventure for a good man some would even dare to die. But God commendeth his love toward us, in that, while we were yet sinners, Christ died for us." - Romans 5:7-8

"Enter ye in at the strait gate: for wide is the gate, and broad is the way, that leadeth to destruction, and many there be which go in thereat: Because strait is the gate, and narrow is the way, which leadeth unto life, and few there be that find it." - Matthew 7:13-14

"Whom having not seen, ye love; in whom, though now ye see him not, yet believing, ye rejoice with joy unspeakable and full of glory: Receiving the end of your faith, even the salvation of your souls." - 1 Peter 1:8-9

"For so hath the Lord commanded us, saying, I have set thee to be a light of the Gentiles, that thou shouldest be for salvation unto the ends of the earth." - Acts 13:47

"For I am not ashamed of the gospel of Christ: for it is the power of God unto salvation to every one that believeth; to the Jew first, and also to the Greek." - Romans 1:16

"For if, when we were enemies, we were reconciled to God by the death of his Son, much more, being reconciled, we shall be saved by his life." - Romans 5:10

"Thou hast also given me the shield of thy salvation: and thy right hand hath holden me up, and thy gentleness hath made me great. Thou hast enlarged my steps under me, that my feet did not slip." - Psalm 18:35-36

"For God sent not his Son into the world to condemn the world; but that the world through him might be saved." - John 3:17

"In God is my salvation and my glory: the rock of my strength, and my refuge, is in God." - Psalm 62:7

"For by grace are ye saved through faith; and that not of yourselves: it is the gift of God: Not of works, lest any man should boast." - Ephesians 2:8-9

"For whosoever shall call upon the name of the Lord shall be saved." - Romans 10:13

"I am the door: by me if any man enter in, he shall be saved, and shall go in and out, and find pasture." - John 10:9

"He that hath the Son hath life; and he that hath not the Son of God hath not life." - 1 John 5:12

GOD'S PROMISES AND ASSURANCES

"For God so loved the world, that he gave his only begotten Son, that whosoever believeth in him should not perish, but have everlasting life." - John 3:16

"For the preaching of the cross is to them that perish foolishness; but unto us which are saved it is the power of God." - 1 Corinthians 1:18

"Wherefore he is able also to save them to the uttermost that come unto God by him, seeing he ever liveth to make intercession for them." - Hebrews 7:25

"But he that shall endure unto the end, the same shall be saved." - Matthew 24:13

"A new heart also will I give you, and a new spirit will I put within you: and I will take away the stony heart out of your flesh, and I will give you an heart of flesh." - Ezekiel 36:26

"For the Lord is our judge, the Lord is our lawgiver, the Lord is our king; he will save us." - Isaiah 33:22

"Not by works of righteousness which we have done, but according to his mercy he saved us, by the washing of regeneration, and renewing of the Holy Ghost." - Titus 3:5

"The Lord redeemeth the soul of his servants: and none of them that trust in him shall be desolate." - Psalm 34:22

"For I know that this shall turn to my salvation through your prayer, and the supply of the Spirit of Jesus Christ." - Philippians 1:19

"Salvation belongeth unto the Lord: thy blessings is upon thy people. Selah." - Psalm 3:8

"For as by one man's disobedience many were made sinners, so by the obedience of one shall many be made righteous." - Romans 5:19

"As far as the east is from the west, so far hath he removed our transgressions from us." - Psalm 103:12

"Therefore I will look unto the Lord; I will wait for the God of my salvation: my God will hear me." - Micah 7:7

"For whosoever will save his life shall lose it; but whosoever shall lose his life for my sake and the gospel's the same shall save it." - Mark 8:35

"I have blotted out, as a thick cloud, thy transgressions, and, as a cloud, thy sins: return unto me; for I have redeemed thee." - Isaiah 44:22

"And being made perfect, he became the author of eternal salvation unto all them that obey him." - Hebrews 5:9

Faith, Faithful, And Faithfulness

The Bible teaches that faith is the key for the Christian walk. It is by faith we believe in God and accepts Jesus Christ as the only Begotten Son of God. The Bible tells us "without faith it is impossible to please God." Our faith unlocks the door to eternity for us.

What is faith? Faith is the confident, assurance that what we hope for is going to happen. It is the evidence of things we cannot see. By faith, we believe that the universe was formed at God's command. By faith, we believe that everything that exist is what God created, including us. Faith is the foundation of our relationship with God. Faith is believing what God did and what He says He will do, in the Bible.

The New Testament describes four facets of faith, Saving Faith, Action Faith, Keeping Faith, and the Gift of Faith. Saving Faith, is where it all begins, just by believing. Action Faith, is putting your feet to your faith. Keeping Faith, is a continuous trust in God and

His promises. The Gift of Faith, is a special gift from God's Holy Spirit. The Holy Spirit produces faithfulness in us.

"Know therefore that the Lord your God is God, the faithful God who keeps covenant and steadfast love with those who love him and keep his commandments, to a thousand generations." - Deuteronomy 7:9

"But the Lord is faithful. He will establish you and guard you against the evil one." - 2 Thessalonians 3:3

"There hath no temptaion taken you but such is common to man: but God is faithful, who will not suffer you to be temped above that ye are able; but will with the temptation also make a way to escape, that ye may be able to bear it." - 1 Corinthians 10:13

"If we confess our sins, he is faithful and just to forgive us our sins and to cleanse us from all unrighteousness." - 1 John 1:9

"God is faithful, by whom you were called into the fellowship of his Son, Jesus Christ our Lord." - 1 Corinthians 1:9

"Let us hold fast the confession of our hope without wavering, for he who promised is faithful." - Hebrews 10:23

"God is not man, that he should lie, or a son of man, that he should change his mind, Has he said, and will he not do it? Or has he spoken, and will he not fulfill it?" - Numbers 23:19

"It is of the Lord's mercies that we are not consumed, because his compassions fail not. They are new every morning: great is thy faithfulness." - Lamentations 3:22-23

"For the word of the Lord is upright, and all his work is done in faithfulness." - Psalm 33:4

"For what if some did not believe? shall their unbelief make the faith of God without effect?" - Romans 3:3

"But you, O Lord, are a God mericful and gracious, slow to anger and abounding in steadfast love and faithfulness." - Psalm 86:15

"The Lord passed before him and proclaimed, "The Lord, the Lord, a God merciful and gracious, slow to anger, and abounding in steadfast love and faithfulness." - Exodus 34:6

"A faithful man will abound with blessings, but whoever hastens to be rich will not go unpunished." - Proverbs 28:20

"He will cover you with his pinions, and under his wings you will find refuge; his faithfulness is a shield and buckler." - Psalm 91:4

"O Lord God of hosts, who is mighty as you are, O Lord, with your faithfulness all around you?" - Psalm 89:8

"Thy mercy, O Lord, is in the heavens: and thy faithfulness reacheth unto the clouds." - Psalm 36:5

"Through faith also Sara herself received strength to conceive seed, and was delivered of a child when she was past age, because she judged him faithful who had promised." - Hebrews 11:11

"Faithful is he that calleth you, who also will do it." - 1 Thessalonians 5:24

"I have not hid thy righteousness within my heart; I have declared thy faithfulness and thy salvation: I have not concealed thy lovingkindness and thy truth from the great congregation." - Psalm 40:10

"Wherefore let them that suffer according to the will of God commit the keeping of their souls to him in well doing, as unto a faithful Creator." - 1 Peter 4:19

"But without faith it it impossible to please him: for he that cometh to God must believe that he is, and that he is a rewarder of them that diligently seek him." - Hebrews 11:6

"O Lord, thou art my God; I will exalt thee, I will praise thy name; for thou hast done wonderful things; thy counsels of old are faithfulness and truth." - Isaiah 25:1

"Thy faithfulness is unto all generations: thou hast established the earth, and it abideth." - Psalms 119:90

"But the fruit of the Spirit is love, joy, peace, longsuffering, gentleness, goodness, faith, Meekness, temperance: against such there is no law." - Galatians 5:22-23

"And he said unto him, Well thou good servant: because thou hast been faithful in a very little, have thou authority over ten cities." - Luke 19"17

"Now faith is the substance of things hoped for, the evidence of things not seen." - Hebrews 11:1

"Hear my prayer, O Lord, give ear to my supplications: in thy faithfulness answer me, and in thy righteousness." - Psalm 143:1

"He that is faithful in that which is least is faithful also in much: and he that is unjust in the least is unjust also in much." - Luke 16:10

"Nevertheless my lovingkindness will I not utterly take from him, nor suffer my faithfulness to fail." - Psalm 89:33

"And the very God of peace sanctify you wholly; and I pray God your whole spirit and soul and body be preserved blameless unto the coming or our Lord Jesus Christ. Faithfyl is he that calleth you, who also will do it." - 1 Thessalonians 5:23-23

"Fear none of those things which thou shalt suffer: behold, the devil shall cast some of you into prison, that ye may be tried; and

ye shall have tribulation ten days: be thou faithful unto death, and I will give thee a crown of life." - Revelation 2:10

"Knowing that a man is not justified by the works of the law, but by the faith of Jesus Christ, even we have believed in Jesus Christ, that we might be justified by the faith of Christ, and not by the works of the law; for by the works of the law shall no flesh be justified." - Galatians 2:16

"O love the Lord, all ye his saints: for the Lord preserveth the faithful, and plentifully rewardeth the proud doer." - Psalm 31:23

"Who was faithful to him that appointed him, as also Moses was faithful in all his house." - Hebrews 3:2

"And the Lord said, Who then is that faithful and wise steward, whom his lord shall make ruler over his household, to give them their portion of meat in due season? Blessed us that servant whom his lord when he cometh shall find so doing. Of a truth I say unto you, that he will make him ruler over all that he hath." - Luke 12:42-44

"And I saw heaven opened, and behold a white horse; and he that sat upon him was called Faithful and True, and in righteousness he doth judge and make war." - Revelation 19:11

"I will sing of the mercies of the Lord for ever: with my mouth will I make known thy faithfulness to all generations. For I have said,

Mercy shall be built up for ever: thy faithfulness shalt thou establish in the very heavens." - Psalm 89:1-2

"I know, O Lord, that thy judgments are right, and that thou in faithfulness hast afflicted me." - Psalm 119:75

"And unto the angel of the church of the Laodiceans write; faithful and true witness, the beginning of the creation of God." - Revelations 3:14

"For therein is the righteousness of God revealed from faith to faith: as it is written, The just shall live by faith." - Romans 1:17

"And from Jesus Christ, who is the faithful witness, and the first begotten of the dead, and the prince of the kings of the earth. Unto him that loved us, and washed us from our sins in his own blood." - Revelations 1:5

"He that is faithful in that which is least is faithful also in much: and he that is unjust in the least is unjust also in much. If therefore ye have not been faithful in the unrighteous mammon, who will commit to your trust the true riches? And if ye have not been faithful in that which is another man's who shall give you that which is your own?" - Luke 16:10-12

"Therefore being justified by faith, we have peace with God through our Lord Jesus Christ; By whom also we have access by faith into this grace wherein we stand, and rejoice in hope of the glory of God. And not only so, but we glory in tribulations also:

knowing that tribulation worketh patience; And patience, experience; and experience, hope: And hope maketh not ashamed; because the love of God is shed abroad in our hearts by the Holy Ghost which is given unto us." - Romans 5:1-5

"For we walk by faith, not by sight." - 2 Corinthians 5:7

Peace And Comfort

What is "Peace" in the Bible? The peace of God is different from the peace of the world. Biblical peace is more than a state of tranquility. It is more than the absence of violence. Jesus is the symbol of "peace" and "comfort." He is our peace with God and He provides us with comfort.

Biblical peace is not something that we can get on our own. It is a fruit of the Spirit. God is the Source of all peace. His name is Peace, Yahweh Shalom, which means the Lord is Peace. Jesus is the Prince of Peace and only He can give peace.

"Blessed be God, even the Father of our Lord Jesus Christ, the Father of mercies, and the God of all comfort; Who comforteth us in all our tribulation, that we may be able to comfort them which are in any trouble, by the comfort wherewith we ourselves are comforted of God." - 2 Corinthians 1:3-4

"It is of the Lord's mercies that we are not consumed, because his compassions fail not. They are new every morning: great is thy faithfulness." - Lamentations 3:22-23

"As ye know how we exhorted and comforted and charged every one of you, as a father doth his children, That ye would walk worthy of God, who hath called you unto his kingdom and glory."
- 1 Thessalonians 2:11-12

"God is our refuge and strength, a very present help in trouble. Therefore will not we fear, though the earth be removed, and though the mountains be carried into the midst of the sea; Though the waters thereof roar and be troubled, though the mountains shake with the swelling thereof. Selah." - Psalm 46:1-3

"Yea, though I walk through the valley of the shadow of death, I will fear no evil: for thou art with me; thy rod and thy staff they comfort me." - Psalm 23:4

"Trust in the Lord with all thine heart; and lean not unto thine own understanding. In all thy ways acknowledge him, and he shall direct thy paths." - Proverbs 3:5-6

"But they that wait upon the Lord shall renew their strength; they shall mount up with wings as eagles; they shall run, and not be weary; and they shall walk, and not faint." - Isaiah 40:31

"Come unto me, all ye that labour and are heavy laden, and I will give you rest. Take my yoke upon you, and learn of me; for I am meek and lowly heart: and ye shall find rest unto your souls. For my yoke is easy, and my burden is light." - Matthew 11:28-30

"Fear thou not; for I am with thee: be not dismayed; for I am thy God: I will strengthen thee; yea, I will help thee; yea, I will uphold thee with the right hand of my righteousness." - Isaiah 41:10

"The Lord also will be a refuge for the oppressed, a refuge in times of trouble." - Psalm 9:9

"The Lord is good, a strong hold in the day of trouble; and he knoweth them that trust in him." - Nahum 1:7

"The righteous cry, and the Lord heareth, and delivereth them out of all their troubles." - Psalm 34:17

"Now unto him that is able to do exceeding abundantly above all that we ask or think, according to the power that worketh in us." - Ephesians 3:20

"Have not I commanded thee? Be strong and of a good courage; be not afraid, neither be thou dismayed: for the Lord thy God is with thee whithersoever thou goest." - Joshua 1:9

"I can do all things through Christ which strengtheneth me." - Philippians 4:13

"For this God is our God for ever and ever: he will be our guide even unto death." - Psalm 48:14

"Who comforteth us in all our tribulation, that we may be able to comfort them which are in any trouble, by the comfort wherewith we ourselves are comforted of God." - 2 Corinthians 1:4

"Be strong and of good courage, fear not, nor be afraid of them: for the Lord thy God, he it is that doth go with thee; he will not fail thee, nor forsake thee." - Deuteronomy 31:6

"Be of good courage, and he shall strengthen your heart, all ye that hope in the Lord." - Psalm 31:24

"Finally, brethren, farewell. Be perfect, be of good comfort, be of one mind, live in peace; and the God of love and peace shall be with you." - 2 Corinthians 13:11

"Blessed are they that mourn: for they shall be comforted." - Matthew 5:4

"And the peace of God, which passeth all understanding, shall keep your hearts and minds through Christ Jesus." - Philippians 4:7

"What shall we then say to these things? If God be for us, who can be against us?" - Romans 8:31

"For God hath not given us the spirit of fear; but of power, and of love, and of a sound mind." - 2 Timothy 1:7

"Cast thy burden upon the Lord, and he shall sustain thee: he shall never suffer the righteous to be moved." - Psalm 55:22

"Now the God of hope fill you with all joy and peace in believing, that ye may abound in hope, through the power of the Holy Ghost." - Romans 15:13

"Thou wilt keep him in perfect peace, whose mind is stayed on thee: because he trusteth in thee. Trust ye in the Lord for ever: for in the Lord Jehovah is everlasting strength." - Isaiah 26:3-4

"The Lord is nigh unto them that are of a broken heart; and saveth such as be of a contrite spirit." = Psalm 34:18

"Heaven and earth shall pass away, but my words shall not pass away." - Matthew 24:35

"O taste and see that the Lord is good: blessed is the man that trusteth in him." - Psalm 34:8

"I, even I, am he that comforteth you: who are thou, that thou shouldest be afraid of a man that shall die, and of the son of man which shall be made as grass." - Isaiah 51:12

"He that believeth on me, as the scripture hath said, out of his belly shall flow rivers of living water." - John 7:38

"And God shall wipe away all tears from their eyes; and there shall be no more death, neither sorrow, nor crying, neither shall there be any more pain: for the former things are passed away." - Revelation 21:4

"He healeth the broken in heart, and bindeth up their wounds." - Psalm 147:3

"Peace I leave with you, my peace I give unto you: not as the world giveth, give I unto you. Let not your heart be troubled, neither let it be afraid." - John 14:27

"Which hope we have as an anchor of the soul, both sure and stedfast, and which entereth into that within the veil." - Hebrews 6:19

"Depart from evil, and do good; seek peace, and pursue it." - Psalm 34:14

"But my God shall supply all your need according to his riches in glory by Christ Jesus." - Philippians 4:19

"Now our Lord Jesus Christ himself, and God, even our Father, which hath loved us, and hath given us everlasting consolation and good hope through grace, Comfort your hearts, and stablish you in every good word and work." - 2 Thessalonians 2:16-17

"And my people shall dwell in a peaceable habitation, and in sure dwellings, and in quiet resting places." - Isaiah 32:18

"The Lord will give strength unto his people; the Lord will bless his people with peace." Psalm 29:11

GOD'S PROMISES AND ASSURANCES

"Now the God of hope fill you with all joy and peace in believing, that ye may abound in hope, through the power of the Holy Ghost." - Romans 15:13

"There us no peace, saith my God, to the wicked." - Isaiah 57:21

"For whatsoever things were written aforetime were written for our learning, that we through patience and comfort of the scriptures might have hope." - Romans 15:4

"I create the fruit of the lips; Peace, peace to him that is far off, and to him that is near, saith the Lord; and I will heal him." - Isaiah 57:19

"And hope maketh not ashamed; because the love of God is shed abroad in our hearts by the Holy Ghost which is given unto us." - Romans 5:4

"For the kingdom of God is not meat and drink; but righteousness, and peace, and joy in the Holy Ghost." - Romans 14:17

"For as the sufferings of Christ abound in us, so our consolation also aboundeth by Christ." 2 Corinthians 1:5

"These things I have spoken unto you, that in me ye might have peace. In the world ye shall have tribulation: but be of good cheer; I have overcome the world." - John 16:33

Wisdom

"Wisdom is more precious than rubies, and nothing you desire can compare with her."

Wisdom is the ability to think and act using knowledge, experience, understanding, insight, and common sense. Wisdom is not the same thing as knowledge. Wisdom is more than common sense. Experience alone isn't enough.

Fear of the Lord is the beginning of wisdom. Wisdom comes from God, and is a very real and pratical sense of what to do, how to do it, and why it must be done. Wisdom is a gift from God.

A person who is wise is someone with the ability to see what is happening, appraise what has happened, anticipate what may happen, knows how to evaluate which course of action to take, then make the very best decision. But this discernment can't come from you by yourself. You can only obtain wisdom through God.

Christ is the Wisdom. To fear the Lord is the beginning of wisdom, and God can begin to provide us with wisdom through

Jesus. "And because of him, you are in Christ Jesus, who became to us wisdom from God righteousness and sanctification, and redemption."

"And I have filled him with the spirit of God, in wisdom, and in understanding, and in knowledge, and in all manner of workmanship." - Exodus 31:3

"To know wisdom and instruction; to perceive the words of understanding." - Proverbs 1:2

"If any of you lacks wisdom, let him ask God, who gives generously to all without reproach, and it will be given him." - James 1:5

"Behold, thou desireth truth in the inward parts: and in the hidden part thou shalt make me to know wisdom." - Psalm 51:6

"Happy are thy men, happy are these thy servants, which stand continually before thee, and that hear thy wisdom." - 1 Kings 10:8

"To receive the instruction of wisdom, justice, and judgment, and equity." - Proverbs 1:3

"Let the word of Christ dwell in you richly, teaching and admonishing one another in all wisdom, singing psalms and hymns and spiritual songs, with thankfulness in your hearts to God." - Colossians 3:16

"So teach us to number our days, that we may apply our hearts unto wisdom." - Psalm 90:12

"And that he would show thee the secrets of wisdom, that they are double to that which is! Know therefore that God exacteth of thee less than thine iniquity deserveth." - Job 11:6

"The fear of the Lord is the beginning of knowledge: but fools despise wisdom and instruction." - Proverbs 1:7

"The mouth of the righteous speaketh wisdom, and his tongue talketh of judgment." - Psalm 37:30

"But the wisdom from above is first pure, then peaceable, gentle, open to reason, full of mercy and good fruits, impartial and sincere." - James 3:17

"With the ancient is wisdom; and in length of days understanding." - Job 12:12

"For the Lord giveth wisdom: out of his mouth cometh knowledge and understanding. He layeth up sound wisdom for the righteous: he is a buckler to them that walk uprightly." - Proverbs 2:6-7

"The fear of the Lord is the beginning of wisdom: a good understanding have all they that do his commandments: his priase endureth for ever." - Psalm 111:10

"And so, from the day we heard, we have not ceased to pray for you, asking that you may be filled with the knowledge of his will in all spiritual wisdom and understanding." - Colossians 1:9

"Happy is the man that findeth wisdom, and the man that getteth understanding." - Proverbs 3:13

"For to the one who pleases him God has given wisdom and knowledge and joy, but to the sinner he has given the business of gathering and collecting, only to give to one who pleases God. This also is vanity and a striving after wind." - Ecclesiastes 2:26

"O that ye would altogether hold your peace! and it should be your wisdom." - Job 13:5

"And because of him you are in Christ Jesus, who became to us wisdom from God, righteousness and sanctification and redemption." - 1 Corinthians 1:30

"When wisdom entereth into thine heart, and knowledge is pleasant unto thy soul." - Proverbs 2:10

"Anf unto man he said, Behold, the fear of the Lord, that is wisdom; and to depart from evil is understanding." - Job 28:28

"For your obedience is known to all, so that I rejoice over you, but I want you to be wise as to what is good and innocent as to what is evil." - Romans 16:19

"Whoever is wise, let him attend to these things; let them consider the steadfast love of the Lord." - Psalm 107:43

"Him we proclaim, warning everyone and teaching everyone with all wisdom, that we may present everyone mature in Christ." - Colossians 1:28

"My son, let not them depart from thine eyes: keep sound wisdom and discreation." - Proverbs 3:21

"For the protection of wisdom is like the protection of money, and the advantage of knowledge is that wisdom preserves the life of him who has it." - Ecclesiastes 7:12

"Get wisdom, get understanding: forget it not; neither decline from the words of my mouth." - Proverbs 4:5

"That their hearts may be encouraged, being knit together in love, to reach all the riches of full assurance of understanding and the knowledge of God's mystery, which is Christ, in whom are hidden all the treasures of wisdom and knowledge." - Colossians 2"2-3

"Wisdom is the principal thing: therefore get wisdom: and with all thy getting get understanding." - Proverbs 4:7

"For to one is given through the Spirit the utterance of wisdom, and to another the utterance of knowledge according to the same Spirit." - 1 Corinthians 12:8

"For wisdom is better than rubies; and all the things that may be desired are not to be compared to it." - Proverbs 8:11

"For although they knew God, they did not honor him as God or give thanks to him, but they became futile in their thinking, and their foolish hearts were darkened. Claiming to be wise, they became fools, and exchanged the glory of the immortal God for images resembling mortal man and birds and animals and creeping things." - Romans 1:21-23

"By insolence comes nothing but strife, but with those who take advice is wisdom." - Proverbs 13:10

"But wisdom is justified of all her children." - Luke 7:35

"When the Spirit of truth comes, he will guide you into all the truth, for he will not speak on his own authority, but whatever he hears he will speak, and he will declare to you the things that are to come." - John 16:13

"For the foolishness of God is wiser than men, and the weakness of God is stronger than man." - 1 Corinthians 1:25

"Give instruction to a wise man, and he will be still wiser; teach a righteous man, and he will increase in learning." - Proverbs 9:9

"Which things also we speak, not in the words which man's wisdom teacheth, but which the Holy Ghost teacheth; comparing spiritual things with spiritual." - 1 Corinthians 2:13

"And wisdom and knowledge shall be the stability of thy times, and strength of salvation: the fear of the Lord is his treasure." Isaiah 33:2

"Trust in the Lord with all your heart, and do not lean on your own understanding. In all your ways acknowledge him, and he will make straight your paths. Be not wise in your own eyes; fear the Lord, and turn away from evil." - Proverbs 3:5-7

"And he changeth the times and the season: he removeth kings, and setteth up kings: he giveth wisdom unto the wise, and knowledge to them that know understanding." - Daniel 2:21

"The mouth of the righteous utters wisdom, and his tongue speaks justice." - Psalm 37:30

"That the God of our Lord Jesus Christ, the Father of glory, may give unto you the spirit of wisdom and revelation in the knowledge of him." - Ephesians 1:17

"Howbeit we speak wisdom among them that are perfect: yet not the wisdom of this world, nor of the princes of this world, that come to nought." - 1 Corinthians 2:6

"How much better to get wisdom than gold! To get understanding is to be chosen rather than silver." - Proverbs 16:16

"For I will give you a mouth and wisdom, which all your adversaries shall not be able to gainsay nor resist." - Luke 21:15

"Wisdom rests in the heart of a man of understanding, but it makes itself known even in the midst of fools." - Proverbs 14:33

Joy

Joy is a Fruit of the Spirit. God, Himself, is the originator of this spiritual fruit, called joy. God is the only One that can produce joy and He does it through His Spirit that dwells within those who put their trust in Him.

You can find joy even in adversity. Yes, even in difficult times it may seem hard to be joyful, but the Scriptures clearly tells us that, "weeping may endure for a night, but joy cometh in the morning."

Apostle Paul says, "consider it pure joy…whenever you face trails." This is not some joy, but complete and full joy, from the Lord. It's joy at its fullest. So whatever your challenges are in life, only through God can you discover and have this authentic joy in every season of your life.

"Thou wilt shew me the path of life: in thy presence is fulness of joy; at thy right hand there are pleasures for evermore." - Psalm 16:11

"Rejoice in the Lord always: and again I say, Rejoice." - Philippians 4:4

"For his anger endureth but a moment; in his favour is life: weeping may endure for a night, but joy cometh in the morning." - Psalm 30:5

"Whom having not seen, ye love; in whom, though now ye see him not, yet believing, ye rejoice with joy unspeakable and full of glory: Receiving the end of your faith, even the salvation of your souls." - 1 Peter 1:8-9

"I say unto you, that likewise joy shall be in heaven over one sinner that repenteth, more than over ninety and nine just persons, which need no repentance." - Luke 15:7

"And ye now therefore have sorrow: but I will see you again, and your heart shall rejoice, and your joy no man taketh from you. And in that day ye shall ask me nothing. Verily, verily, I say unto you, Whatsoever ye shall ask the Father in my name, he will give it you. Hitherto have ye asked nothing in my name: ask, and ye shall receive, that your joy may be full." - John 16:22-24

"These things have I spoken unto you, that my joy might remain in you, and that your joy might be full." - John 15:11

"He that handleth a matter wisely shall find good: and whoso trusteth in the Lord, happy is he." - Proverbs 16:20

"They that sow in tear shall reap in joy." - Psalm 126:5

"The father of the righteous shall greatly rejoice: and he that begetteth a wise child shall have joy in him." - Proverbs 23:24

"Therefore with joy shall ye draw water out of the wells of salvation." - Isaiah 12:3

"And now come I to thee; and these things I speak in the world, that they might have my joy fulfilled in themselves." - John 17:13

"For the kingdom of God is not meat and drink; but righteousness, and peace, and joy in the Holy Ghost." - Romans 14:17

"Rejoice ye in that day, and leap for joy: for behold, your reward is great in heaven: for in the like manner did their fathers unto the prophets." - Luke 6:23

"And the ransomed of the Lord shall return, and come to Zion with songs and everlasting joy upon their heads: they shall obtain joy and gladness, and sorrow and sighing shall flee away." - Isaiah 35:10

"For what is our hope, or joy, or crown or rejoicing? Are not even ye in the presence of our Lord Jesus Christ at his coming?" - 1 Thessalonians 2:19

"But rejoice, inasmuch as ye are partakers of Christ's sufferings; that when his glory shall be revealed, ye may be glad also with exceeding joy." - 1 Peter 4:13

"As sorrowful, yet alway rejoicing; as poor, yet making many rich; as having nothing, and yet possessing all things." - 2 Corinthians 6:10

"I will greatly rejoice in the Lord, my soul shall be joyful in my God; for he hath clothed me with the garments of salvation, he hath covered me with the robe of righteousness, as a bridegroom decketh himself with ornaments, and as a bride adorneth herself with her jewels." - Isaiah 61:10

"And ye became followers of us, and of the Lord, having received the word in much affliction, with joy of the Holy Ghost." - 1 Thessalonians 1:6

"I have no greater joy than to hear that my children walk in truth." - 3 John 1:4

"This is the day which the Lord hath made; we will rejoice and be glad in it." - Psalm 118:24

"If there be therefore any consolation in Christ, if any comfort of love, if any fellowship of the Spirit, if any bowels and mercies, Fulfil ye my joy, that ye be likeminded, having the same love, being of one accord, of one mind." - Philippians 2:1-2

"But the fruit of the Spirit is love, joy, peace, longsuffering, gentleness, goodness, faith, Meekness, temperance: against such there is not law." - Galatians 5:22-23

"Looking unto Jesus the author and finisher of our faith; who for the joy that was set before him endured the cross, despising the shame, and is set down at the right hand of the throne of God." - Hebrews 12:2

"For ye shall go out with joy, and be led forth with peace: the mountains and the hills shall break forth before you into singing, and all the trees of the field shall clap their hands." - Isaiah 55:12

"Thou hast put gladness in my heart, more than in the time that their corn and their wine increased." - Psalm 4:7

"But let all those that put their trust in thee rejoice: let them ever shout for joy, because thou defendest them: let them also that love thy name be joyful in thee." Psalm 5:11

"Thy words were found, and I did eat them; and thy word was unto me the joy and rejoicing of mine heart: for I am called by thy name, O Lord God of hosts." - Jeremiah 15:16

"Rejoicing in hope; patient in tribulation; continuing instant in prayer." - Romans 12:12

"Then he said unto them, Go your way, eat the fat, and drink the sweet, and send portions unto them for whom nothing is prepared: for this day is holy unto our Lord: neither be ye sorry; for the joy of the Lord is your strength." - Nehemiah 8:10

"My brethren, count it all joy when ye fall into divers temptaions." - James 1:2

"Now the God of hope fill you with all joy and peace in believing, that ye may abound in hope, through the power of the Holy Ghost." - Romans 15:13

"Restore unto me the joy of thy salvation; and uphold me with thy free spirit." - Psalm 51:12

"Rejoice evermore. Pray without ceasing. In every thing give thanks: for this is the will of God in Christ Jesus concerning you." 1 Thessalonians 5:16-18

"O clap your hands, all ye people; shout unto God with the voice of truimph." - Psalm 47:1

"The Lord thy God in the midst of thee is mighty; he will save, he will rejoice over thee with joy; he will rest in his, he will joy thee with singing." - Zephaniah 3:17

"A man hath joy by the answer of his mouth: and a word spoken in due season, how good is it!" - Proverbs 15:23

"My lips shall greatly rejoice when I sing unto thee; and my soul, which thou hast redeemed." - Psalm 71:23

"O come, let us sing unto the Lord: let us make a joyful noise to the rock of our salvation. Let us come before his presence with

thanksgiving, and make a joyful noise unto him with psalms."
- Psalm 95:1-2

"For ye are our glory and joy." - 1 Thessalonians 2:20

"For we have great joy and consolation in thy love, because the bowels of the saints are refreshed by thee, brother." - Philemon 1:7

"And there were in the same country shepherds abiding in the field, keeping watch over their flock by night. And, lo, the angel of the Lord came upon them, and the glory of the Lord shone round about them: and they were sore afraid. And the angel said unto them, Fear not: for, behold, I bring you good tidings of great joy, which shall be to all people. For unto you is born this day in the city of David a Saviour, which is Christ the Lord."
- Luke 2:8-11

"And now shall mine head be lifted up above mine enemies round about me: therefore will I offer in his tabernacle sacrifices of joy; I will sing, yea, I will sing praises unto the Lord." - Psalm 27:6

"And the seventy returned again with joy, saying, Lord, even the devils are subject unto us through thy name." - Luke 10:17

"Be glad in the Lord, and rejoice, ye righteous: and shout for joy, all ye that are upright in heart." - Psalm 32:11

"Obey them that have the rule over you, and submit yourselves: for they watch for your souls, as they that must give account, that they may do it with joy, and not with grief: for that is unprofitable for you." - Hebrews 13:17

"Thy testimonies have I taken as an heritage for ever: for they are the rejoicing of my heart." - Psalm 119:111

"Rejoice with them that do rejoice, and weep with them that weep." - Romans 12:15

"Thou hast made known to me the ways of life; thou shalt make me full of joy with thy countenance." - Acts 2:28

"Always in every prayer of mine for you all making request with joy, For your fellowship in the gospel from the first day until now." - Philippians 1:4-5

"Let all those that seek thee rejoice and be glad in thee: and let such as love thy salvation say continually, Let God be magnified." - Psalm 70:4

"For I rejoiced greatly, when the brethren came and testified of the truth is in thee, even as thou walkest in the truth. I have no greater joy than to hear that my children walk in truth." - 3 John 1: 3-4

""Then was our mouth filled with laughter, and our tongue with singing: then said they among the heathen, The Lord hath done great things for them. The Lord hath done great things for us; whereof we are glad." - Psalm 126:2-3

"I have rejoiced in the way of thy testimonies, as much as in all riches." - Psalm 119:14

"And my spirit hath rejoiced in God my Saviour." - Luke 1:47

"Now unto him that is able to keep you from falling, and to present you faultless before the presence of his glory with exceeding joy, To the only wise God our Saviour, be glory and majesty, dominion and power, both now and ever. Amen." - Jude 1:24-25

"Make a joyful noise unto the Lord, all ye lands." - Psalm 100:1

"I will be glad and rejoice in thee: I will sing praise to thy name, O thou most High." - Psalm 9:2

"In the day of prosperity be joyful, but in the day of adversity consider: God also hath set the one over against the other, to the end that man should find nothing after him." - Ecclesiastes 7:14

"Whom having not seen, ye love: in whom, though now ye see with joy unspeakable and full of glory: Receiving the end of your faith, even the salvation of your souls." - 1 Peter 1:8-9

"My brethren, count it all joy when ye fall into divers temptations; Knowing this, that the trying of your faith worketh patience. But let patience have her perfect work, that ye may be perfect and entire, wanting nothing." - James 1:2-4

"Therefore my heart is glad, and my glory rejoiceth: my flesh also shall rest in hope." - Psalm 16:9

"Rejoice evermore." - 1 Thessalonians 5:16

"For our heart shall rejoice in him, because we have trusted in his holy name." - Psalm 33:21

"That I may come unto you with joy by the will of God, and may with you be refreshed." - Romans 15:32

"The statues of the Lord are right, rejoicing the heart: the commandment of the Lord is pure, enlightening the eyes." - Psalm 19:8

"His lord said unto him, Well done, thou good and faithful servant: thou hast been faithful over a few things, I will make thee ruler over many things: enter thou into the joy of thy lord." - Matthew 25:21

"Make me to hear joy and gladness; that the bones which thou hast broken may rejoice." - Psalm 51:8

"And they worshipped him, and returned to Jerusalem with great joy." - Luke 24:52

"In thy name shall they rejoice all the day: and in thy righteousness shall they be exalted." Psalm 89:16

"As sorrowful, yet always rejoicing; as poor, yet making many rich; as having nothing, and yet possessing all things." - 2 Corinthians 6:10

"They that sow in tears shall reap in joy. He that goeth forth and weepeth, bearing precious seed, shall doubtless come again with rejoicing, bringing his sheaves with him." Psalm 126:5-6

"Not for that we have dominion over your faith, but are helpers of your joy: for thy faith ye stand." - 2 Corinthians 1:24

"And not only so, but we also joy in God through our Lord Jesus Christ, by whom we have now received the atonement." - Romans 5:11

"For what thanks can we render to God again for you, for all the joy wherewith we joy for your sakes before our God." - 1 Thessalonians 3:9

"And the disciples were filled with joy, and with the Holy Ghost." - Acts 13:52

Love

Jesus said, "I give you a new commandment, that you love one another, Just as I have loved you, you also should love one another." That's it! It is just that simple. We are to love ALL People! Even those who hurt you, those who breaks your heart, those who lie on you, those who deceive you, those who can't do nothing for you, even those that seems impossible to love.

Love is an emotion characterized by intimacy, passion, and commitment. Biblical or divine love is a self-sacrificing, caring, commitment that shows itself in seeking the highest good for the one being loved.

Biblical love is a caring commitment. It is not just duty, it involves delight. This caring commitment is not an attitude, it requires action. It shows itself in deeds and often requires some sacrifice. The ulimate demonstration of self-sacrificing commitment and love was Jesus, when He sacrificed Himself on the cross ay Calvary. This was the highest good of the One who truly loves.

We should love one another because love is from God. God's love was revealed among us in this way: God sent His only Son into this sin filled world, so that we might live through Him. To love one another is evidence of God, it is revealing that God is abiding in us.

"For God so loved the world, that he gave his only begotten Son, that whosoever believeth in him should not perish, but have everlasting life." - John 3:16

"With all lowliness and meekness, with longsuffering, forbearing one another in love; Endeavouring to keep the unity of the Spirit in the bond of peace." - Ephesians 4:2-3

"And above all these things put on charity, which is the bond of perfectness." - Colossians 3:14

"Charity suffereth long, and is kind; charity envieth not; charity vaunteth not itself, is not puffed up, Doth not behave itself unseemly, seeketh not her own, is not easily provoked, thinketh no evil; Rejoiceth not in iniquity, but rejoiceth in the truth; Beareth all things, believeth all things, hopeth all things, endureth all things. Charity never faileth: but whether there be prophecies, they shall fail; whether there be tongues, they shall cease; whether there be knowledge, it shall vanish away." - 1 Corinthians 13:4-8

"He that loveth not knoweth not God; for God is love." - 1 John 4:8

"Know therefore that the Lord thy God, he is God, the faithful God, which keepeth covenant and mercy with them that love him and keep his commandments to a thousand generations." - Deuteronomy 7:9

"Husbands, love your wives, even as Christ also loved the church, and gave himself for it." - Ephesians 5:25

"Let all your things be done with charity." - 1 Corinthians 16:14

"For I am persuaded, that neither death, nor life, nor angels, nor principalities, nor powers, nor things present, nor things to come, Nor height, nor depth, nor any other creature, shall be able to separate us from the love of God, which is in Christ Jesus our Lord." - Romans 8:38-39

"Jesus said unto him, Thous shalt love the Lord thy God with all thy heart, and with all thy soul, and with all thy mind. This is the first and great commandment. And the second is like unto it, Thou shalt love thy neighbour as thyself." - Matthew 22: 37-39

"Beloved, let us love one another: for love is of God; and every one that loveth is born of God, and knoweth God. He that loveth not knoweth not God; for God is love." - 1 John 4:7-8

"The Lord hath appeared of old unto me, saying Yea, I have loved thee with an everlasting love: therefore with lovingkindness have I drawn thee." - Jeremiah 31:3

"Set me as a seal upon thine heart, as a seal upon thine arm: for love is strong as death; jealousy is cruel as the grave: the coals thereof are coals of fire, which hath a most vehement flame. Many waters cannot quench love, neither can the floods drown it: if a man would give all the substance of his house for love, it would utterly be contemned." - Song of Solomon 8:6-7

"And above all things have fervent charity among yourselves: for charity shall cover the multitude of sins." - 1 Peter 4:8

"But God commendeth his love toward us, in that, while we were yet sinners, Christ died for us." - Romans 5:8

"And now abideth faith, hope, charity, these three; but the greatest of these is charity." - 1 Corinthians 13:13

"Let not mercy and truth forsake thee: bind them about thy neck; write them upon the table of thine heart: So shalt thou find favour and good understanding in the sight of God and man." - Proverbs 3:3-4

"And we have known and believed the love that God is love; and he that dwelleth in love dwelleth in God, and God in him. Herein is our love made perfect, that we may have boldness in the day of judgment: because as he is, so are we in this world. There is no fear in love; but perfect love casteth out fear: because fear hath torment. He that feareth is not made perfect in love." - 1 John 4:16-18

"Owe no man any thing, but to love one another: for he that loveth another hath fulfilled the law." - Romans 13:8

"In this was manifested the love of God toward us, because that God sent his only begotten Son into the world, that we might live through him. Herein is love, not that we loved God, but that he loved us, and sent his Son to be the propitiation for our sins. Beloved, if God so loved us, we ought also to love one another." - 1 John 4:9-11

"A new commandment I give unto you, That ye love one another; as I have loved you, that ye also love one another. By this shall all men know that ye are my disciples, if ye have love one to another." - John 13:34-35

"I am crucified with Christ: nevertheless I live; yet not I, but Christ liveth in me: and the life which I now live in the flesh I live by the faith of the Son of God, who loved me, and gave himself for me." - Galatians 2:20

"The Lord thy God in the midst of thee is mighty; he will save, he will rejoice over thee with joy; he will rest in his love, he will joy over thee with singing." - Zephaniah 3:17

"Let love be without dissimulation. Abhor that which is evil; cleave to that which is good." - Romans 12:9

"Greater love hath no man than this, that a man lay down his life for his friends." - John 15:13

"Hatred stirreth up strifes: but love covereth all sins." - Proverbs 10:12

"Hereby perceive we the love of God, because he laid down his life for us: and we ought to lay down our lives for the brethren." - 1 John 3:16

"There is nor fear in love; but perfect love casteth out fear: because fear hath torment. He that feareth is not made perfect in love. We love him, because he first loved us." - 1 John 4:18-19

"But God, who is rich in mercy, for his great love wherewith he loved us, Even when we were dead in sins, hath quickened us together with Christ, (by grace ye are saved;)." - Ephesians 2:4-5

"Behold, what manner of love the Father hath bestowed upon us, that we should be called the sons of God: therefore the world knoweth us not, because it knew him not." 1 John 3:1

"A friend loveth at all times, and a brother is born for adversity." - Proverbs 17:17

"My beloved is mine, and I am his: he feedeth among the lilies." - Song of Solomon 2:16

"And Jesus answered him, The first of all the commandments is, Hear, O Israel; The Lord our God is one Lord: And thou shalt love the Lord thy God with all thy heart, and with all thy soul, and with all thy mind, and with all thy strength: this is the first commandment. And the second is like, namely this, Thou shalt love thy neighbour as thyself. There is none other commandment greater than these." - Mark 12:29-31

"He that getteth wisdom loveth his own soul: he that keepeth understanding shall find good." - Proverbs 19:8

"And he answering said, Thou shalt love the Lord thy God with all thy heart, and with all thy soul, and with all thy strength, and with all thy mind; and thy neighbour as thyself." - Luke 10:27

"This is my commandment, That ye love one another, as I have loved you." - John 15:12

"That Christ may dwell in your hearts by faith; that ye, being rooted and grounded in love, May be able to comprehend with all saints what is the breadth, and length, and depth, and height; And to know the love of Christ, which passeth knowledge, that ye might be filled with all the fulness of God." - Ephesians 3:17-19

"But I say unto you which hear, Love your enemies, do good to them which hate you, Bless them that curse you, and pray for them which despitefully use you. And unto him that smiteth thee on the one cheek offer also the other; and him that taketh away thy cloak forbid not to take thy coat also. Give to every man that asketh of thee; and of him that taketh away thy goods ask them not again. And as ye would that men should do to you, do ye also to them likewise." - Luke 6:27-31

"Because thy lovingkindness is better than life, my lips shall praise thee." - Psalm 63:3

"And though I have the gift of prophecy, and understand all mysteries, and all knowledge; and though I have all faith, so that I could remove mountains, and have not charity, I am nothing." - 1 Corinthians 13:2

"As the Father hath loved me, so have I loved you: continue ye in my love. If ye keep my commandments, ye shall abide in my love; even as I have kept my Father's commandments, and abide in his love." - John 15:9-10

"Be kindly affectioned one to another with brotherly love; in honour preferring one another." - Romans 12:10

"For the Lord loveth judgment, and forsaketh not his saints; they are preserved for ever: but the seed of the wicked shall be cut off." Psalm 37:28

"And the Lord direct your hearts into the love of God, and into the patient waiting for Christ." - 2 Thessalonians 3:5

"How excellent is thy lovingkindness, O God! therefore the children of men put their trust under thy shadow of thy wings." - Psalm 36:7

"If ye love me, keep my commandments." - John 14:15

"But love ye your enemies, and do good, and lend, hoping for nothing again; and your reward shall be great, and ye shall be the children of the Highest: for he is kind unto the unthankful and to the evil." - Luke 6:35

"Who shall separate us from the love of Christ? shall tribulation, or distress, or persecution, or famine, or nakedness, or peril, or sword? As it is written, For thy sake we are killed all the day long; we are accounted as sheep for the slaughter. Nay, in all these things we are more than conquerors through him that loved us. For I am persuaded, that neither death, nor life, nor angels, nor principalities, nor powers, nor things present, nor things to come, Nor height, nor depth, nor any other creature, shall be able to separate us from the love of God, which is in Christ Jesus or Lord." - Romans 8:35-39

"No man hath seen God at any time, If we love one another, God dwelleth in us, and his love is perfected in us." - 1 John 4:12

"Have mercy upon me, O God, according to thy lovingkindness; according unto the multitude of they tender mercies blot out my transgressions." - Psalm 51:1

"I love them that love me; and those that seek me early shall find me." - Proverbs 8:17

"And not only so, but we glory in tribulations also: knowing that tribulation worketh patience; And patience, experience; and experience, hope: And hope maketh not ashamed; because the love of God is shed abroad in our hearts by the Holy Ghost which is given unto us." - Romans 5:3-5

"As the Father hath loved me, so have I loved you: continue ye in my love." - John 15:9

"For whom the Lord loveth he chasteneth, and scourgeth every son whom he receiveth." - Hebrews 12:6

"And walk in love, as Christ also hath loved us, and hath given himself for us an offering and a sacrifice to God for a sweetsmelling savour." - Ephesians 5:2

"And this commandment have we from him, That he also loveth God love his brother also." - 1 John 4:21

"But the fruit of the Spirit is love, joy, peace, longsuffering, gentleness, goodness, faith, Meekness, temperance: against such there is no law." - Galatians 5:22-23

"And we know that all things work together for good to them that love God, to them who are the called according to his purpose." - Romans 8:28

Shelter And Refuge

God is our shelter and refuge. He is our safe place. He is our shelter of protection from trouble and danger. Even when we are stressed, sad, tired, lonely, fearful, disappointed, or discouraged. Life is full of problems. Sometimes we become so focused on the problems, we overlook the fact the we can give those problems to the Problem Solver. We should have confidence in God, who is our divine Protector and Deliver.

Did not God make us many promises? Did not the Psalmist say that those who, "dwell in the shelter of the Most High will rest in the shadow of the Almighty?" We are to seek refuge under God's wings and be assured of His protection. Have you not read the promise that no harm will overtake you because God will command His angels to protect you? Did not God promise to give you the desires of your hearts? Surely, God knows your every thought, I am sure He would be more than willing to help His own, especially when you need relief from suffering of any kind.

"He that dwelleth in the secret place of the most High shall abide under the shadow of the Almighty. I will say of the Lord,

He is my refuge and my fortress: my God: in him will I trust."
- Psalm 91:1-2

"There will be a shelter to give shade from the heat by day, and refuge and protection from the storm and the rain." - Isaiah 4:6

"If we have food and covering, with these we shall be content."
- 1 Timothy 6:8

"From the end of the earth will I cry unto thee, when my heart is overwhelmed: lead me to the rock that is higher than I. For thou hast been a shelter for me, and a strong tower from the enemy."
- Psalm 61:2-3

"The name of the Lord is a strong tower; the righteous runneth into it, and is safe." - Proverbs 18:10

"The Lord is my rock and my fortress and my deliverer, My God, my rock, in whom I take refuge; My shield and the horn of my salvation, my stronghold." - Psalm 18:2

"Speak to the children of Israel, saying, Appoint out for you cities of refuge, whereof I spake unto you by the hand of Moses."
- Joshua 20:2

"Because thou hast made the Lord, which is my refuge, even the most High, thy habitation; There shall no evil befall thee, neither shall any plague some nigh thy dwelling. For he shall give his angels charge over thee, to keep thee in all thy ways." - Psalm 91:9-13

"Every word of God is tested; He is a shield to those who take refuge in Him." - Proverbs 30:5

"You hide them in the secret place of Your presence from the conspiracies of man; You keep them secretly in a shelter from the strifes of tongues." - Psalm 31:20

"God is our refuge and strength, A very present help in trouble." - Psalm 46:1

"For thou hast been a strength to the poor, a strength to the needy, in his distress, a refuge from the storm, a shadow from the heat, when the blast of the terrible ones is as a storm against the wall." - Isaiah 26:4

"I cried unto thee, O Lord: I said, Thou art my refuge and my portion in the land of the living." - Psalm 142:5

"Trust in him at all times; ye people, pour out your heart before him: God is a refuge for us. Selah." - Psalm 62:8

"The God of my rock; in him will I trust, he is my shield, and the horn of my salvation, my high tower, and my refuge; my saviour, thou savest me from violence." - 2 Samuel 22:3

"It is better to take refuge in the Lord than to trust in man." - Psalm 118:8

"O taste and see that the Lord is good; How blessed is the mand who takes refuge in Him!" - Psalm 34:8

"The Lord is good, A stronghold in the day of trouble, And He know those who take refuge in Him." - Nahum 1:7

"He will cover you with His pinions, And under His wings you may seek refuge; His faithfulness is a shield and bulwark." - Psalm 91:4

"For in the time of trouble He will hide me in his pavilion; in the secret of his tabernacle shall he hide me; he shall set me up upon a rock." - Psalm 27:5

"May the Lord reward your work, and your wages be full from the Lord, the God of Israel, under whose wings you have come to seek refuge." - Ruth 2:12

"For You have been a refuge for me, A tower of strength against the enemy." - Psalm 61:3

"As for God, His way is blameless; The word of the Lord is tried; He is a shield to all who take refuge in Him." - Psalm 18:30

"Because ye have said, We have made a covenant with death, and with hell are we at agreement; when the overflowing scourge shall pass through, it shall not come unto us: for we have made lies our refuge, and under falsehood have we hid ourselves." - Isaiah 28:15

GOD'S PROMISES AND ASSURANCES

"Surely goodness and mercy shall follow me all the days of my life; and I will dwell in the house of the Lord for ever." - Psalm 23:6

"The Lord also will be a refuge for the oppressed, a refuge in times of trouble." - Psalm 9:9

"As for God, his way is perfect; the word of the Lord is tried: he is a buckler to all them that trust in him." - 2 Samuel 22:31

"But I will sing of thy power; yea, I will sing aloud of thy mercy in the morning: for thou hast been my defence and refuge in the day of my trouble." - Psalm 59:16

"I am as a wonder unto many; but thou art my strong refuge." - Psalm 71:7

"That by two immutable things, in which it was impossible for God to lie, we might have a strong consolation, who have fled for refuge to lay hold upon the hope set before us." - Hebrews 6:18

""But the LORD is my defence; and my God is the rock of my refuge." - Pslam 94:22

"In the fear of the Lord is strong confidence: and his children shall have a place of refuge." - Proverbs 14:26

"And there shall be a tabernacle for a shadow in the daytime from the heat, and for a place of refuge, and for a covert from storm and from rain." - Isaiah 4:6

"O LORD, my strength, and my fortress, and my refuge in the day of affliction, the Gentiles shall come unto thee from the ends of the earth, and shall say, Surely our fathers have inherited lies, vanity, and things wherein there is no profit." - Jeremiah 16:19

Deliverance From Evil

"And lead us not into temptation, but deliver us from evil." The Lord's Prayer is meant to be an example of prayer. When we pray, "deliver us from evil." we are praying for everything that wretches havoc in our lives. Against all the wickedness, cunning, against sin, from the devil and mankind.

When we pray, "deliver us from evil," we are saying, deliver us from the evil one, acknowledging that there is evil in this world and it is under the control by a supreme evilness. "We know that we are children of God, and that the whole world is under the control of the evil one" (1John 5:19).

But have no fear! God is Sovereign and He is in control of all things and everything. As believers in Jesus, He has equipped us for such a time as this. He will give you everything you need to perform His calling and purpose. We must hold fast to the faith, believing in Jesus' promises and the Truth. The One who made the promises is faithful. We must not be fearful, but faithful.

"And he said unto them, When ye pray, say, Our Father which art in heaven, Hallowed be thy name. Thy kingdom come. Thy will be done, as in heaven, so in earth. Give us this day by day our daily bread. And forgive us our sins; for we alos forgive every one that is indebted to us. And lead us not into temptation; but deliver us from evil." - Luke 11:2-4

"No weapon that is formed against thee shall prosper; and every tongue that shall rise against thee in judgment thou shalt condemn. This is the heritage of the servants of the Lord, and their righteousness is of me, saith the LORD." - Isaiah 54:17

"There shall no evil befall thee, neither shall any plague come nigh thy dwelling. For he shall give his angels charge over thee, to keep thee in all thy ways." - Psalm 91:10-11

"But the Lord is faithful, who shall stablish you, and keep you from evil." - 2 Thessalonians 3:3

"That we should be saved from our enemies, and from the hand of all that hate us." - Luke 1:71

"And the Lord shall deliver me from every evil work, and will preserve me unto his heavenly kingdom: to whom be glory for ever and ever. Amen." - 2 Timothy 4:18

"For we wrestle not against flesh and blood, but against principalities, against powers, against the rulers of the darkness of this world, against spiritual wickedness in high places. Wherefore take unto you the whole armour of God, that ye may be able to withstand in the evil day, and having done all to stand." - Ephesians 6:12-13

"The fear of the Lord tendeth to life: and he that hath it shall abide satisfied; he shall not be visited with evil." - Proverbs 19:23

"And it shall come to pass, if thou shalt hearken diligently unto the voice of the LORD thy God, to observe and do all his commandments which I command thee this day, that the LORD thy God will set thee on high above all nations of the earth: And all these blessings shall come on thee, and overtake thee, if thou shalt hearken unto the voice of the LORD thy God. Blessed shalt thou be in the city, and blessed shalt thou be in the field. Blessed shall be the fruit of thy body, and the fruit of thy ground, and the fruit of thy cattle, the increase of thy kine, and the flocks of thy sheep. Blessed shall be thy basket and thy store. Blessed shalt thou be when thou comest in, and blessed shalt thou be when thou goest out. The LORD shall cause thine enemies that rise up against thee to be smitten before thy face: they shall come out against thee one way, and flee before thee seven ways." - Deuteronomy 28:1-7

"And that we may be delivered from unreasonable and wicked men; for all men have not faith." - 2 Thessalonians 3:2

"Forasmuch as ye know that ye were not redeemed with corruption things, as silver and godl, from your vain conversation received by tradition from your fathers; But with the precious

blood of Christ, as of a lamb without blemish and without spot."
- 1 Peter 1:18-19

"Though I walk in the midst of trouble, thou wilt revive me: thou shalt stretch forth thine hand against the wrath of mine enemies, and thy right hand shall save me." - Psalm 138:7

"That we henceforth be no more children, tossed to and fro, and carried about with every wind of doctrine, by the sleight of men, and cunning craftiness, whereby they lie in wait to deceive."
- Ephesians 4:14

"Submit yourselves therefore to God, Resist the devil, and he will flee from you." - James 4:7

"Behold, I give unto you power to tread on serpents and scorpions, and over all the power of the enemy: and nothing shall by any means hurt you." - Luke 10:19

"The Lord is my shepherd; I shall not want. He maketh me to lie down in green pastures: he leadeth me beside the still waters. He restoreth my soul: he leadeth me in the paths of righteousness for his name's sake. Yea, though I walk through the valley of the shadow of death, I will fear no evil: for thou are with me; thy rod and thy staff they comfort me. Thou preparest a table before me in the presence of mine enemies: thou anointest my head with oil; Surely goodness and mercy shall follow me all the days of my life: and I will dwell in the house of the LORD for ever."
- Psalm 23:1-6

"Above all, taking the shield of faith, wherewith ye shall be able to quench all the fiery darts of the wicked." - Ephesians 6:16

"The God of my rock; in him will I trust: he is my shield, and the horn of my salvation, my high tower, and my refuge, my saviour; thou savest me from violence. I will call on the Lord, who is worthy to be praised: so shall I be saved from mine enemies." - 2 Samuel 22:3-4

"Submit yourselves therefore to God. Resist the devil, and he will flee from you." - James 4:7

"And the Lord shall help them, and deliver them: he shall deliver them from the wicked, and save them, because they trust in him." - Psalm 37:40

"There hath no temptation taken you but such as is common to man: but God is faithful, who will not suffer you to be tempted above that ye are able; but will with the temptation also make a way to escape, that ye may be able to bear it." - 1 Corinthians 10:13

"God is our refuge and strength, a very present help in trouble." - Psalms 46:1

"And lead us not into temptaion, but deliver us from evil: For thine is the kingdom, and the power, and the glory, for ever. Amen." - Matthew 6:13

"The Lord shall preserve thee from all evil: he shall preserve thy soul." - Psalm 121:7

"That he would grant unto us, that we being delivered out of the hand of our enemies might serve him without fear." - Luke 1:74

"To whom ye forgive any thing, I forgive also: for I forgave it, for your sakes forgave I it in the person of Christ; Lest Satan should get an advantage of us: for we are not ignorant of his devices." - 2 Corinthians 2:10-11

"Finally, my brethren, be strong in the Lord, and in the power of his might. Put on the whole armour of God, that ye may be able to stand against the wiles of the devil." - Ephesians 6:10-11

"He delivered me from my strong enemy, and from them which hated me: for they were too strong for me." - Psalm 18:17

Trouble

God is a very present help in trouble. God is amidst us in all circumstances. When difficult times occur, God promises to be our refuge. If the promises of God are misappropriated or neglected, then how are they able to work in our lives as originally intended? We must stand on God's promises by faith, trusting and believing Him at His Word.

We must be willing to seek refuge in God's will for our lives. His will is our security blanket. When we are consistently following the Lord and doing His will, He places a hedge of protection around us, 24 hours a day, and 7 days a week.

The closer we are to God, the more secure we will become. God not only provides us with His protection, but He strengthens us in every troubling and problematic experience. As He strengthens us, we will grow in faith, love, and hope.

"The LORD also will be a refuge for the oppressed, a refuge in times of trouble. And they that know thy name will put their trust in the: for thou LORD, hast not forsaken them that seek thee." - Palm 9:9-10

"The LORD hear thee in the day of trouble; the name of the God of Jacob defend thee." - Psalm 20:1

"Therefore thou deliveredst them into the hand of their enemies, who vexed them: and in the time of their trouble, when they cried unto thee, thou heardest them from heaven; and according to thy manifold mercies thou gavest them saviours, who saved them out of the hand of their enemies." - Nehemiah 9:27

"For in the time of trouble he shall hide me in his pavilion: in the secret of his tabernacle shall he hide me; he shall set up upon a rock." - Psalm 27:5

"I will be glad and rejoice in thy mercy: for thou hast considered my trouble; thou hast known my soul in adversities." - Psalm 31:7

"Confidence in an unfaithful man in time of trouble is like a broken tooth, and a foot out of joint." - Proverbs 25:19

"Thou are my hiding place; thou shalt preserve me from trouble; thou shalt compass me about with songs of deliverance. Selah." - Psalm 32:7

"Have mercy upon me, O LORD, for I am in trouble: mine eye is consumed with grief, yea, my soul and my belly." - Psalm 31:9

"For the thing which I greatly feared is come upon me, and that which I was afraid of is come unto me. I was not in safety, neither had I rest, neither was I quiet; yet trouble came. " - Job 3:25-26

"My times are in thy hand: deliver me from the hand of mine enemies, and from them that persecute me." - Psalm 31:15

"This poor man cried, and the LORD heard him, and saved him out of all his troubles." - Psalm 34:6

"Although affliction cometh not forth of the dust, neither doth trouble spring out of the ground; Yet man is born unto trouble, as the sparks fly upward." - Job 5:6-7

"The face of the Lord is against them that do evil, to cut off the remembrance of them from the earth. The righteous cry, and the LORD heareth, and delivereth them out of all their troubles." - Psalm 34:16-17

"But the salvation of the righteous is of the Lord: he is their strength in the time of trouble." - Psalm 37:39

"But and if ye suffer for righteousness' sake, happy are ye: and be not afraid of their terror, neither be troubled." - 1 Peter 3:14

""Blessed is he that considereth the poor: the LORD will deliver him in time of trouble. The LORD will preserve him, and keep him alive; and he shall be blessed upon the earth: and thou wilt not deliver him unto the will of his enemies." - Psalm 41:1-2

"Let not your heart be troubled: ye believe in God, believe also in me." - John 14:1

""God is our refuge and stength, a very present help in trouble. Therefore will not we fear, though the earth be removed, and though the mountains be carried into the midst of the sea; Though the waters thereof roar and be troubled, though the mountains shake with the swelling thereof. Selah." - Psalm 46:1-3

"And call upon me in the day of trouble: I will deliver thee, and thou shalt glorify me. But unto the wicked God saith, What hast thou to do to declare my statues, or that thou shouldest take my covenant in thy mouth? - Psalm 50:15-16

"Who shall separate us from the love of Christ? shall tribulation, or distress, or persecution, or famine, or nakedness, or peril, or sword." - Romans 8:35

"For he hath delivered me out of all trouble: and mine eye hath seen his desire upon mine enemies." - Psalm 54:7

"That he who blesseth himself in the earth shall bless himself in the God of truth; and he that sweareth in the earth shall swear by the God of truth; because the former troubles are forgotten, and because they are hid from mine eyes." - Isaiah 65:16

"Give us help from trouble: for vain is the help of man. Through God we shall do valiantly: for he itis that shall tread down our enemies." - Psalm 60:11-12

"Trust in him at all time; ye people, pour out your heart before him: God is a refuge for us. Selah." - Psalm 62:8

"Which my lips have uttered, and my mouth hath spoken, when I was in trouble." - Psalm 66:14

"Blessed be God, even the Father of our Lord Jesus Christ, the Father of mercies, and the God of all comfort; Who comforteth us in all our tribulation, that we may be able to comfort them which are in any trouble, by the comfot wherewith we ourselves are comforted of God." - 2 Corinthians 1:3-4

"Hear me, O LORD; for thy lovingkindness is good: turn unto me according to the multitude of thy tender merices. And Hide not thy face from thy servant; for I am in trouble: hear me speedily." - Psalm 69:16-17

"Thou which hast shewed me great and sore troubles, shalt quicken me again, and shalt bring me up again from the depths of the earth. Thou shalt increase my greatness, and comfort me on every side." - Psalm 71:20-21

"These things I have spoken unto you, that in me ye might have peace. In the world ye shall have tribulation: but be of good cheer; I have overcome the world." - John 16:33

"They are not in trouble as other men; neither are they plagued like other men." - Psalm 73:5

"For nation shall rise against nation, and kingdom against kingdom: and there shall be earthquakes in divers places, and there shall be famines and troubles: these are the beginnings of sorrows." - Mark 13:8

"I cried unto God with my voice, even unto God with my voice; and he gave ear unto me. In the day of my trouble I sought the Lord: my sore ran in the night, and ceased not: my soul refused to be comforted." - Psalm 77:1-2

"For all this they sinned still, and believed not for his wondrous works. Therefor their days did he consume in vanity, and their years in trouble." - Psalm 78:32-33

"He cast upon them the fierceness of his anger, wrath, and indignation, and trouble, by sending evil angels among them." - Psalm 78:49

"Thou calledst in trouble, and I delivered thee; I answered thee in the secret place of thunder: I proved thee at the waters of Meribah. Selah." - Psalm 81:7

"For we wrestle not against flesh and blood, but against principalities, against powers, against the rulers of the darkness of this world, against spiritual wickedness in high places." - Ephesians 6:12

"Give ear, O Lord, unto my prayer; and attend to the voice of my supplications. In the day of my trouble I will call upon thee: for thou wilt answer me." - Psalm 86:6-7

"Because he hath set his love upon me, therefore will I deliver him: I will set him on high, because he hath known my name. He shall call upon me, and I will answer him: I will be with him in trouble; I will deliver him, and honour him." - Psalm 91:14-15

"Hear my prayer, O Lord, and let my cry come unto thee. Hide not thy face from me in the day when I am in trouble; incline thine ear unto me: in the day when I call answer me speedily." - Psalm 102:1-2

"The Lord is good, a strong hold in the day of trouble; and he knoweth them that trust in him." - Hahum 1:7

"Then they cried unto the LORD in their trouble, and he delivered them out of their distresses." - Psalm 107:6

"Then they cried unto the LORD in their trouble, and he saved them out of their distresses." - Psalm 107:13

"Peace I leave with you, my peace I give unto you: not as the world giveth, give I unto you, Let not your heart be troubled, neither let it be afraid." - John 14:27

"Though I walk in the midst of trouble, thou wilt revive me: thou shalt stretch forth thine hand against the wrath of mine enemies, and thy right hand shall save me." - Psalm 138:7

"Better is little with the fear of the Lord than great treasure and trouble therewith." - Proverbs 15:16

"This know also, that in the last days perilous times shall come. For men shall be lovers of their own selves, covetous, boasters, proud, blasphemers, disobedient to parents, unthankful, unholy, Without natural affection, trucebreakers, false accusers, incontinent, fierce, despisers of those that are good, Traitors, heady, highminded, lovers of pleasures more than lovers of God; Having a form of godliness, but denying the power thereof: from such turn away. For this sort are they which creep into houses, and lead captive silly women laden with sins, led away with divers lusts, Ever learning, and never able to come to the knowledge of the truth." - 2 Timothy 3:1-7

Prayer

Prayer is simply, communicating with God. God is always with us and He is always ready to listen to us. The Bible says that we should pray without ceasing. Praying continuously doesn't mean that you are praying 24 hours a day, seven days a week, with your eyes closed and your head bowed. It means you are constantly talking to God and listening to God's voice.

God should be our favorite person to talk to. You can tell Him about your good days and bad days, exciting events and boring events, when you are facing a major decision, or just going on vacation.

God should be the most important person in your life and He desires for you to communicate with Him. Why do we need to let God know what's going on in our life? God is all-knowing, right? He already knows what is going on with you any way. The truth is, God values a relationship with us. We should pray for all occasions, with all kinds of prayers and requests.

When you have a close relationship with God, you will learn to hear His voice and understand His character, in ways you were never able to do before. You will be in constant prayer, but you won't be speaking. There will be a constant communication, going in both directions, with God through prayer.

"And when they had prayed, the place was shaken where they were assembled together; and they were all filled with the Holy Ghost, and they spake the word of God with boldness." - Acts 4:31

"Be careful for nothing; but in every thing by prayer and supplication with thanksgiving let your requests be made known unto God. And the peace of God, which passeth all understanding, shall keep your hearts and minds through Christ Jesus." - Philippians 4:6-7

"Rejoicing in hope; patient in tribulation; continuing instant in prayer." - Romans 12:12

"Verily I say unto you, If ye have faith, and doubt not, ye shall not only do this which is done to the fig tree, but also if ye shall say unto this mountain, Be thou removed, and be thous cast into the sea; it shall be done. And all things, whatsoever ye shall ask in prayer, believing, ye shall receive." - Matthew 21:21-22

"The LORD is nigh unto all them that call upon him, to all that call upon him in truth." - Psalm 145:18

"Ye have not chosen me, but I have chosen you, and ordained you, that ye should go and bring forth fruit, and that your fruit should remain: that whatsoever ye shall ask of the Father in my name, he may give it you." - John 15:16

"Confess your faults on to another, and pray one for another, that ye may be healed. The effectual fervent prayer of a righteous man availeth much." - James 5:16

"And this is the confidence that we have in him, that if we ask any thing according to his will, he heareth us: And if we know that he hear us, whatsoever we ask, we know that we have the petitions that we desired of him." - 1 John 5:14-15

"Therefore I say unto you, What things soever ye desire, when ye pray, believe that ye receive them, and ye shall have them." - Mark 11:24

"Hear my prayer, O LORD, give ear to my supplications: in thy faithfulness answer me, and in thy righteousness." - Psalm 143:1

"And he spake a parable unto them to this end, that men ought always to pray, and not to faint." - Luke 18:1

"Call unto me, and I will answer thee, and shew thee great and mighty things, which thou knowest not." - Jeremiah 33:3

"Again I say unto you, That if two of you shall agree on earth as touching any thing that they shall ask, it shall be done for them of my Father which is in heaven. For where two or three are gathered together in my name, there am I in the midst of them." - Matthew 18:19-20

"And when they had fasted and prayed, and laid their hands on them, they sent them away." - Acts 13:3

"And whatsoever ye shall ask in my name, that will I do that the Father may be glorified in the Son. If ye ask any thing in my name, I will do it." - John 14:13-14

"I called upon the Lord in distress: the Lord answered me, and set me in a large place." - Psalm 118:5

"And I say unto you, Ask, and it shall be given you; and ye shall find; knock, and it shall be opened unto you." - Luke 11:9

"But let him ask in faith, nothing wavering. For he that wavereth is like a wave of the sea driven with the wind and tossed" - James 1:6

"Watch and pray, that ye enter not into temptaion: the spirit indeed is willing, but the fesh is weak." - Matthew 26:41

"And if we know that he hear us, whatsoever we ask, we know that we have the petitions that we desired of him." - 1 John 5:15

"But the end of all things is at hand: be ye therefore sober, and watch unto prayer." - 1 Peter 4:7

"Now we know that God heareth not sinners; but if any man be a worshipper of God, and doeth his will, him he heareth." - John 9:31

"I cried unto him with my mouth, and he was extolled with my tongue." - Psalm 66:17

"I exhort therefore, that, first of all, supplications, prayers, intercessions, and giving of thanks, be made for all men." - 1 Timothy 2:1

"Is any among you afflicted? let him pray. Is any merry? let him sing psalms." - James 5:13

"Peter therefore was kept in prison: but prayer was made without ceasing of the church unto God for him." - Acts 12:5

"Pray without ceasing. In every thing give thanks: for this is the will of God in Christ Jesus concerning you." - 1 Thessalonians 5:17-18

"Yet the Lord will command his lovingkindness in the daytime, and in the nigh his song shall be with me, and my prayer unto the God of my life." Psalm 42:8

"Continue in prayer also, and watch in the same with thanksgiving." - Colossians 4:2

"If ye abide in me, and my words abide in you, ye shall ask what ye will, and it shall be done unto you." - John 15:7

"And it came to pass in those days, that he went out into a mountain to pray, and continued all night in prayer to God."
- Luke 6:12

"Watch and pray, that ye enter not into temptation: the spirit indeed is willing, but the flesh is weak." - Matthew 26:41

"And the prayer of faith shall save the sick, and the Lord shall raise him up; and if he have committed sins, they shall be forgiven him."
- James 5:15

"And when ye stand praying, forgive, it ye have ought against any: that your Father also which is in heaven may forgive you your trepasses." - Mark 11:25

"My voice shalt thou hear in the morning, O Lord; in the morning will I direct my prayer unto thee, and will look up."
- Psalm 5:3

"Is any sick among you? let him call for the elders of the church; and let them pray over him, anointing him with oil in the name of the Lord." - James 5:14

"We give thanks to God and the Father of our Lord Jesus Christ, praying always for you." - Colossians 1:3

"Let my prayer be set forth before thee as incense; and the lifting up of my hands as the evening sacrifice." - Psalm 141:2

"But I say unto you, Love your enemies, bless them that curse your, do good to them that hate you, and pray for them which despitefully use you, and persecute you." - Matthew 5:44

"Who in the days of his flesh, when he had offered up prayers and supplications with strong crying and tears unto him that was able to save him from death, and was heard in that he feared." - Hebrews 5:7

"For I know that this shall turn to my salvation through your prayer, and the supply of the Spirit of Jesus Christ." - Philippians 1:19

"But I say unto you which hear, Love your enemies, do good to them which hate you, Bless them that curse you, and pray for them which despitefully use you." - Luke 6:27-28

"The righteous cry, and the LORD heareth, and delivereth them out of all their troubles." - Psalm 34:17

"Praying always with all prayer and supplication in the Spirit, and watching thereunto with all perservance and supplication for all saints." - Ephesians 6:18

"After this manner therefore pray ye: Our Father which art in heaven, Hallowed be thy name. Thy kingdom come. Thy will be done in earth, as it is in heaven. Give us this day our daily bread, And forgive us our debts, as we forgive our debtors. And lead

us not into temptation, but deliver us from evil: For thine is the kingdom, and the power, and the glory, for ever. Amen."
- Matthew 6:9-15

"Likewise the Spirit also helpeth our infirmities: for we know not what we should pray for as we ought: but the Spirit itself maketh intercession for us with groanings which cannot be uttered. And he that searcheth the hearts knoweth what is the mind of the Spirit, because he maketh intercession for the saints according to the will of God." - Romans 8:26-27

"But when ye pray, use not vain repetitions, as the heathen do: for they think that they shall be heard for their much speaking."
- Matthew 6:7

"Now when all the people were baptized, it came to pass, that Jesus also being baptized, and praying, the heaven was opened, And the Holy Ghost descended in a bodily shape like a dove upon him, and a voice came from heaven, which said, Thou art my beloved Son; in thee I am well pleased." - Luke 3:21-22

"Therefore I say unto you, What things soever ye desire, when ye pray, believe that ye receive them, and ye shall have them."
- Mark 11:24

"But ye, beloved, building up yourselves on your most holy faith, praying in the Holy Ghost." - Jude 1:20

"For the eyes of the Lord are over the righteous and his ears are open unto their prayers: but the face of the Lord is against them that do evil." - 1 Peter 3:12

"And they continued stedfastly in the apostles doctrine and fellowship, and in breaking of bread, and in prayers." - Acts 2:42

"Watch ye therefore, and pray always, that ye may be accounted worthy to escape all these things that shall come to pass, and to stand before the Son of man." - Luke 21:36

"And in the morning, rising up a great while before day, he went out, and departed into a solitary place, and there prayed." - Mark 1:35

"But thou, when thou prayest, enter into thy closet, and when thou hast shut thy door, pray to thy Father which is in secret; and thy Father which seeth in secret shall reward thee openly." - Matthew 6:6

"And it came to pass, that, as he was praying in a certain place, when he ceased, one of his disciples said unto him, Lord, teach us to pray, as John also taught his disciples. And he said unto them, When ye pray, say, Hallowed be thy name, Thy kingdom come. Thy will be done, as in heaven, so in earth. Give us day by day our daily bread. And forgive us our sins; for we also forgive every one that is indebted to us. And lead us not into temptation; but deliver us from evil." - Luke 11:1-4

Secrets And Mysteries

We all have secrets. But why do we keep secrets? For a number of reasons. It could be out of shame or discretion. Most people have "skeletons in their closet." We don't want them revealed because we would feel embarrased or ashamed. God keeps secrets too. There are things that are hidden from us. "The secret things belong to the Lord our God." There are somethings we may never know until we reach our heavenly home.

Mysteries are more than secrets. Mysteries are anything kept secret or remains unexplained or unknown. The Bible used the term "mystery" to refer to a sacred secret. Paul wrote about the mystery of the Gentiles, or non-Jews, becoming part of the Church. This mystery has been made known, encompasses all of what God is doing in and through Christ.

It is Christ in you. It is Christ, Himself. It is the Gospel of Christ. It is the teaching of the Gospel. It is godliness that is received from knowing Christ. It is the Trinity: God is both three and yet One. It is about the depth of His love for us, that we can't comprehend or fathom. It is the Revelation. It is God's judgments poured out upon the earth.

"For there is nothing hid, which shall not be manifested; neither was any thing kept secret, but that it should come abroad." - Mark 4:22

"Shall not God search this out? for he knoweth the secrets of the heart." - Psalm 44:21

"That thou appear not unto men to fast, but unto thy Father which is in secret: and thy Father, which seeth in secret, shall reward thee openly." - Matthew 6:18

"The secret things belong unto the LORD our God: but those things which are revealed belong unto us and to our children for ever; that we may do all the words of this law." - Deutoronomy 29:29

"For it is a shame even to speak of those things which are done of them in secret." - Ephesians 5:12

"Therefore judge nothing before the time, until the Lord come, who both will bring to light the hidden things of darkness, and will make manifest the counsels of the hearts: and then shall every man have praise of God." - 1 Corinthians 4:5

"A gift in secret pacifieth anger: and a reward in the bosom strong wrath." - Proverbs 21:14

"But when his brethren were gone up, then went he also up unto the feast, not openly, but as it were in secret." - John 7:10

"He sitteth in the lurking places of the villages: in the secret places doth he murder the innocent: his eyes are privily set against the poor." - Psalm 10:8

"Now to him that is of power to stablish you according to my gospel, and the preaching of Jesus Christ, according to the revelation of the mystery, which was kept secret since the world began. But now is made manifest, and by the scriptures of the prophets, according to the commandment of the everlasting God, made known to all nations for the obedience of faith." - Romans 16:25-26

"Are the consolations of God small with thee? is there any secret thing with thee?" - Job 15:11

"But thou, when thou prayest, enter into thy closet, and when thou hast shut thy door, pray to thy Father which is in secret; and thy Father which seeth in secret shall reward thee openly." - Matthew 6:6

"For in the time of trouble he shall hide me in his pavilion: in the secret of his tabernacle shall he hide me; he shall set me up upon a rock." - Psalm 27:5

"O that thou wouldest hide me in the grave, that thou wouldest keep me secret, until thy wrath be past, that thou wouldest appoint me a set time, and remember me!" - Job 14:13

"For there is no man that doeth any thing in secret, and he himself seeketh to be known openly. If thou do these things, show thyself to the world." - John 7:4

"Thou hast set our iniquities before thee, our secret sins in the light of thy countenance." - Psalm 90:8

"Wherefore if they shall say unto you, Behold, he is in the desert; go not forth: behold, he is in the secret chambers; believe it not." - Matthew 24:26

"For the froward is abomination to the LORD: but his secret is with the righteous." - Proverbs 3:32

"He that dwelleth in the secret place of the most High shall abide under the shadow of the Almighty. I will say of the LORD, He is my refuge and my fortress: my God; in him will I trust." - Psalm 91:1-2

"For nothing is hidden that will not be made manifest, nor is anything secret that will not be known and come to light." - Luke 8:17

"At that time Jesus answered and said, I thank thee, O Father, LORD of heaven and earth, because thou hast hid these things from the wise and prudent, and hast revealed them unto babes." - Matthew 11:25

"Hast thou heard the secret of God? and dost thou restrain wisdom to thyself?" - Job 15:8

"But there is a God in heaven who reveals mysteries, and he has made known to King Nebuchadnezzar what will be in the latter days. Your dream and the visions of your head as you lay in bed are these." - Daniel 2:28

"Cursed be the man that maketh any graven or molten image, and abomination unto the LORD, the work of the hands of the craftsman, and putteth it in a secret place. And all the people shall answer and say, Amen." - Deuteronomy 27:15

"That it might be fulfilled which was spoken by the prophet, saying, I will open my mouth in parables; I will utter things which have been kept secret from the foundation of the world." - Matthew 13:35

"Open rebuke is better than secret love." - Proverbs 27:5

"Jesus answered him, I spake openly to the world; I ever taught in the synagogue, and in the temple, whither the Jews always resort; and in secret have I said nothing." - John 18:20

"Come ye near unto me, hear ye this; I have not spoken in secret from the beginning; from the time that it was, there am I: and now the Lord GOD, and his Spirit, hath sent me." - Isaiah 48:16

"Neither is there any creature that is not manifest in his sight: but all things are naked and opened unto the eyes of him with whom we have to do." - Hebrews 4:13

"He made darkness his secret place; his pavilion round about him were dark waters and thick clouds of the skies." - Psalm 18:11

"He answered and said unto them, Because it is given unto you to know the mysteries of the kingdom of heaven, but to them it is not given." - Matthew 13:11

"It is the glory of God to conceal things, but the glory of kings is to search things out." - Proverbs 25:2

"These things God has revealed to us through the Spirit. For the Spirit searches everything, even the depths of God." - 1 Corinthians 2:10

"For God shall bring every work into judgment, with every secret thing, whether it be good, or whether it be evil." - Ecclesiastes 12:14

"And I will give thee the treasures of darkness, and hidden riches of secret places, that thou mayest know that I, the LORD, which call thee by thy name, am the God of Israel." - Isaiah 45:3

Thou shalt hide them in the secret of thy presence from the pride of man: thou shalt keep them secretly in a pavilion from the stife of tongues." - Psalm 31:20

"All darkness shall be hid in his secret places: a fire not blown shall consume him; it shall go ill with him that is left in his tabernacle." - Job 20:26

"For there is nothing covered, that shall not be revealed; neither hid, that shall not be known. Therefore whatsoever ye have spoken in darkness shall be heard in the light; and that which ye have spoken in the ear in closets shall be proclaimed upon the housetops." - Luke 12:2-3

"Debate thy cause with thy neighbour himself; and discover not a secret to another." - Proverbs 25:9

"Whereby, when ye read, ye may understand my knowledge in the mystery of Christ. Which in other ages was not made known unto the sons of men, as it is now revealed unto his holy apostles and prophets by the Spirit." - Ephesians 3:4-5

"No man, when he hath lighted a candle, putteth it in a secret place, neither under a bushel, but on a candlestick, that they which come in may see the light." - Luke 11:33

"The secret of the LORD is with them that fear him; and he will show them his covenant." - Psalm 25:14

"I have not spoken in secret, in a dark place of the earth: I said not unto the seed of Jacob, Seek ye me in vain: I the LORD speak righteousness, I declare things that are right." - Isaiah 45:19

"For the invisible things of him from the creation of the world are clearly seen, being understood by the things that are made, even his eternal power and Godhead; so that they are without excuse." - Romans 1:20

"Can any hide himself in secret places that I shall not see him? saith the LORD. Do not I fill heaven and earth? saith the LORD." - Jeremiah 23:24

"He revealeth the deep and secret things: he knoweth what is in the darkness, and the light dwelleth with him." - Daniel 2:22

"And it was so, that, after they had carried it about, the hand of the LORD was against the city with a very great destruction: and he smote the men of the city, boty small and great, and they had emerods in their secret parts." - 1 Samuel 5:9

"Surely the Lord GOD will do nothing, but he revealeth his secret unto his servants the prophets." - Amos 3:7

"That thine alms may be in secret: and thy Father which seeth in secret himself shall reward thee openly." - Matthew 6:4

"My substance was not hid from thee, when I was made in secret, and curiously wrought in the lowest parts of the earth." - Psalm 139:15

"And the angel of the LORD said unto him, Why askest thou thus after my name, seeing it is secret?" - Judges 13:18

"In the day when God shall judge the secrets of men by Jesus Christ according to my gospel." - Romans 2:16

"Hide me from the secret counsel of the wicked; from the insurrection of the workers of iniquity." - Psalm 64:2

"O my soul, come not thou into their secret; unto their assembly, mine honour, be not thou united: for in ther anger they slew a man, and in their selfwill they digged down a wall." - Genesis 49:6

"But Jonathan Saul's son delighted much in David: and Jonathan told David, saying, Saul my father seeketh to kill thee: now therefore, I pray thee, take heed to thyself until the morning, and abide in a secret place, and hide thyself." - 1 Samuel 19:2

"How that by revelation he made known unto me the mystery; as I wrote afore in few words." - Ephesians 3:3

"Thou hast set our iniquities before thee, our secret sins in the light of thy countenance." - Psalm 90:8

"Therefore judge nothing before the time, until the Lord come, who both will bring to light the hidden things of darkness, and will make manifest the counsels of the hearts: and then shall every man have praise of God." - 1 Corinthians 4:5

"For God shall bring every work into judgment, with every secret things, whether it be good, or whether it be evil." - Ecclesiastes 12:14

"Call unto me, and I will answer thee, and shew thee great and mighty things, which thou knowest not." - Jeremiah 33:3

"Then was the secret revealed unto Daniel in a night vision. Then Daniel blessed the God of heaven." - Daniel 2:19

"And he said, Unto you it is given to know the mysteries of the kingdom of God: but to others in parables; that seeing they might not see, and hearing they might not understand." - Luke 8:10

"And for me, that utterance may be given unto me, that I may open my mouth boldly, to make known the mystery of the gospel." - Ephesians 6:19

"Men and brethren, this scripture must needs have been fulfilled, which the Holy Ghost by the mouth of Davud spake before concerning Judas, which was guide to them that took Jesus." - Acts 1:16

"Henceforth I call you not servants; for the servant knoweth not what his lord doeth: but I have called you friends; for all things that I have heard of my Father I have made known unto you." - John 15:15

"But as it is written, Eye hath not seen, nor ear heard, neither have entered into the heart of man, the things which God hath prepared for them that love him." - 1 Corinthians 2:9

"For this cause shall a man leave his father and mother, and shall be joined unto his wife, and they two shall be one flesh. This is a great mystery: but I speak concerning Christ and the church." - Ephesians 5:31-32

Hope

The definition of hope is a feeling of optimism or a desire that something will happen. Our God is a God of hope. God's hope is looking forward to something with an expectation, benefiting from something good.

Often times, people will place their hope in material things, family, or careers, but disappointingly so, because hope without God is hopelessness.

When we place our hope in God, we know that our life will be one full of enriched blessings. Does this mean that we will not have problems or difficulties? Absolutely not! When the trials of this life come, we can trust God to see us through them. We learn to have peace that surpasses all understanding.

We have an eternal hope, knowing that this world is not our home. We have a Savior who came to give us life and to give it more abundantly.

As Christians, we face trials, but trials develops perservance and character. As our perservance and character is developed, our hope is strengthened.

Our Lord God is faithful and when we hope in Him, we will never be disappointed.

"The Lord taketh pleasure in them that fear him, in those that hope in his mercy." - Psalm 147:11

"Now faith is the substance of things hoped for, the evidence of things not seen." - Hebrews 11:1

"And not only so, but we glory in tribulations also: knowing that tribulation worketh patience; And patience, experience; and experience, hope: And hope maketh not ashamed; because the love of God is shed abroad in our hearts by the Holy Ghost which is given unto us." - Romans 5:3-5

"Let Israel hope in the Lord: for with the Lord there is mercy, and with him is plenteous redemption." - Psalm 130:7

"Wherefore gird up the lions of your mind, be sober, and hope to the end for the grace that is to be brought unto you at the revelation of Jesus Christ." - 1 Peter 1:13

"Now the God of hope fill you with all joy and peace in believing, that ye may abound in hope, through the power of the Holy Ghost." - Romans 15:13

"For our light affliction, which is but for a moment, worketh for us a far more exceeding and eternal weight of glory; While we look not at the things which are seen, but at the things which are not seen: for the things which are seen are temporal; but the things which are not seen are eternal." - 2 Corinthians 4:17-18

"Rejoicing in hope; patient in tribulation; continuing instant in prayer." Romans 12:12

"The eyes of your understanding being enlightened; that ye may know what is hope of his calling, and what the riches of the glory of his inheritance in the saints." - Ephesians 1:18

"That being justified by his grace, we should be made heirs according to the hope of eternal life." - Titus 3:7

"Behold, the eye of the Lord is upon them that fear him, upon them that hope in his mercy." - Psalm 33:18

"And thine age shall be clearer than the noonday: thou shalt shine forth, thou shalt be as the morning. And thou shalt be secure, because there is hope; yea, thou shalt dig about thee, and thou shalt take thy rest in safety. Also thou shalt lie down, and none shall make thee afraid; yea, many shall make suit unto thee." - Job 11:17-19

"Blessed be the God and Father of our Lord Jesus Christ, which according to his abundant mercy hath begotten us again unto a lively hope by the resurrection of Jesus Christ from the dead, To an inheritance incorruptible, and undefiled, and that fadeth not away, reserved in heaven for you." - 1 Peter 1:3-4

"For thou art my hope, O Lord God: thou art my trust from my youth." - Psalm 71:5

"Blessed is the man that trusteth in the Lord, and whose hope the Lord is." - Jeremiah 17:7

"Looking for that blessed hope, and the glorious appearing of the great God and our Saviour Jesus Christ." - Titus 2:13

"Why art thou cast down, O my soul? and why art thou disquieted within me? hope in God: for I shall yet praise him, who is the health of my countenance, and my God." - Psalm 43:5

"The Lord is my portion, saith my soul; therefore will I hope in him." - Lamentations 3:24

"Rejoiceth not in iniquity, but rejoiceth in the truth; Beareth all things, believeth all things, hopeth all things, endureth all things." - 1 Corinthians 13:6-7

"Therefore my heart is glad, and my glory rejoiceth: my flesh also shall rest in hope." - Psalm 16:9

"Blessed be the God and Father of our Lord Jesus Christ, which according to his abundant mercy hath begotten us again unto a lively hope by the resurrection of Jesus Christ from the dead, To

an inheritance incorruptible, and undefiled, and that fadeth not away, reserved in heaven for you." 1 Peter 1:3-4

"But he saveth the poor from the sword, from their mouth, and from the hand of the mighty. So the poor hath hope, and iniquity stoppeth her mouth." - Job 5:15-16

"But I will hope continually, and will yet praise thee more and more." - Psalm 71:13

"Seeing then that we have such hope, we use great plainness of speech: And not as Moses, which put a veil over his face, that the children of Israel could not stedfastly look to the end of that which is abolished: But their minds were blinded: for until this day remaineth the same vail untaken away in the reading of the old testament; which vail is done away in Christ." - 2 Corinthians 3:12-14

"Thou art my hiding place and my shield: I hope in thy word." - Psalm 119:114

"Therefore being justified by faith, we have peace with God through our Lord Jesus Christ: By whom also we have access by faith into this grace wherein we stand, and rejoice in hope of the glory of God." - Romans 5:1-2

"Be of good courage, and he shall strengthen your heart, all ye that hope in the Lord." - Psalm 31:24

"Remembering without ceasing your work of faith, and labour of love, and patience of hope in our Lord Jesus Christ, in the sight of God and our Father." - 1 Thessalonians 1:3

"For the needy shall not always be forgotten: the expectation of the poor shall not perish for ever." - Psalm 9:18

"Who verily was foreordained before the foundation of the world, but was manifest in these last times for you, Who by him do believe in God, that raised him up from the dead, and gave him glory; that your faith and hope might be in God." - 1 Peter 1:20-21

"Why art thou cast down, O my soul? and why art thou disquieted within me? hope thou in God: for I shall yet praise him, who is the health of my countenance, and my God." - Psalm 42:11

"To whom God would make known what is the riches of the glory of this mystery among the Gentiles; which is Christ in you, the hope of glory." - Colossians 1:27

"For whatsoever things were written aforetime were written for our learning, that we through patience and comfort of the scriptures might have hope." - Romans 15:4

"And now, Lord, what wait I for? my hope is in thee." - Psalm 39:7

"If ye continue in the faith grounded and settled, and be not moved away from the hope of the gospel, which ye have heard, and which was preached to every creature which is under heaven; whereof I Paul am made a minister." - Colossians 1:23

"For we are saved by hope: but hope that is seen is not hope: for what a man seeth, why doth he yet hope for? But if we hope for that we see not, then do we with patience wait for it." - Romans 8:24-25

"Turn again, my daughters, go your way; for I am too old to have an husband. If I should say, I have hope, if I should have an husband also to night, and should also bear sons." - Ruth 1:12

"And now abideth faith, hope, charity, these three; but the greatest of these is charity." - 1 Corinthians 13:13

"Let thy mercy, O Lord, be upon us, according as we hope in thee." - Psalm 33:22

"There is one body, and one Spirit, even as ye are called in one hope of your calling; One Lord, one faith, one baptism, One God and Father of all, who is above all, and through all, and in you all." - Ephesians 4:4-6

"I wait for the Lord, my soul doth wait, and in his word do I hope." Psalm 130:5

"And hope maketh not ashamed; because the love of God is shed abroad in our hearts by the Holy Ghost which is given unto us." - Romans 5:5

"Which hope we have as an anchor of the soul, both sure and stedfast, and which entereth into that within the veil." - Hebrews 6:19

"My soul fainteth for thy salvation: but I hope in thy word." - Psalm 119:81

"Now our Lord Jesus Christ himself, and God, even our Father, which hath loved us, and hath given us everlasting consolation and good hope through grace, Comfort your hearts, and stablish you in every good word and work." - 2 Thessalonians 2:16-17

"Paul, a servant of God, and an apostle of Jesus Christ, according to the faith of God's elect, and the acknowledging of the truth which is after godliness; In hope of eternal life, which God, that cannot lie, promised before the world began." - Titus 1:1-2

"But sanctify the Lord God in your hearts: and be ready always to give an answer to every man that asketh you a reason of the hope that is in you with meekness and fear." - 1 Peter 3:15

"But let us, who are of the day, be sober, putting on the breastplate of faith and love; and for an helmet, the hope of salvation." - 1 Thessalonians 5:8

"And every man that hath this hope in him purifieth himself, even as he is pure." - 1 John 3:3

"And where is now my hope? as for my hope, who shall see it?" - Job 17:15

"For we through the Spirit wait for the hope of righteousness by faith." - Galatians 5:5

"But I would not have you to be ignorant, brethren, concerning them which are asleep, that ye sorrow not, even as others which have no hope." - 1 Thessalonians 4:13

"But Christ as a son over his own house; whose house are we, if we hold fast the confidence and the rejoicing of the hope firm unto the end." - Hebrews 3:6

"Paul, an apostle of Jesus Christ by the commandment of God our Saviour, and Lord Jesus Christ, which is our hope." - 1 Timothy 1:1

"Turn you to the strong hold, ye prisoners of hope: even to day do I declare that I will render double unto thee." - Zechariah 9:12

"For the hope which is laid up for you in heaven, whereof ye heard before in the word of the truth of the gospel." - Colossians 1:5

"That they might set their hope in God, and not forget the works of God, but keep his commandments." - Psalm 78:7

"That at that time ye were without Christ, being aliens from the commonwealth of Israel, and strangers from the covenants of promise, having no hope, and without God in the world." - Ephesians 2:12

"And we desire that every one of you do shew the same diligence to the full assurance of hope unto the end." - Hebrews 6:11

"And have hope toward God, which they themselves also allow, that there shall be a resurrection of the dead, both of the just and unjust." - Acts 24:15

"Remembering without ceasing your work of faith, and labour of love, and patience of hope in our Lord Jesus Christ, in the sight of God and our Father." - 1 Thessalonians 1:3

All scriptures quoted from the King James Bible.

Help And Guidance

"Help" is a verb, it is defined: "to give assistance or support to." God promised that He would always be there for us. He would never leave us nor forsake us. He promised to help us in ranges of needs, including trouble, problems, illness, finance, physical, emotional, spiritual, or any conceivable difficulty.

If you ask God for His help, He will give you what you need, even if you don't know what your needs are. But that's okay, because the Holy Spirit that is within us, He understands what our needs are and He communicates it to God, by crying and groaning for us, as He intercedes for us.

God will always be there for us. As He helps us, He guides us. Isn't that so comforting to know. He gave us His Word, the Bible, as a guidebook and it provides us with instructions to live the life that God desires for us. We must trust God to help us and follow where He guides us.

"For this God is our God for ever and ever; he will be our guide even to the end." - Psalm 48:14

"And I will bring the blind by a way that they knew not; I will lead them in paths that they have not known: I will make darkness light before them, and crooked things straight. These things will I do unto them, and not forsake them." - Isaiah 42:16

"For the Lamb which is in the midst of the throne shall feed them, and shall lead them unto living fountains of waters: and God shall wipe away all tears from their eyes." Revelation 7:17

"I am with you and will watch over you wherever you go, and I will bring you back to this land. I will not leave you until I have done what I promised you." - Genesis 28:15

"Have I not commanded you? Be strong and courageous. Do not be afraid; do not be discouraged, for the Lord your God will be with you wherever you go." - Joshua 1:9

"Though he may stumble, he will not fall, for the Lord upholds him with his hand." - Palm 37:4

"Your word is a lamp to guide my feet and a light for my path." - Psalm 119:105

"For I am the Lord your God who takes hold of your right hand and says to you, Do not fear; I will help you." - Isaiah 41:13

"The Lord says, 'I will guide you along the best pathway for your life. I will advise you and watch over you." - Psalm 32:8

"Those who know your name trust in you, for you, Lord, have never forsaken those who seek you." - Psalm 9:10

"In all your ways submit to him and he will make your paths straight." - Proverbs 3:6

"And thine ears shall hear a word behind thee, saying, This is the way, walk ye in it, when ye turn to the right hand, and when ye turn to the left." - Isaiah 30:21

"The Lord will guide you always; he will satisfy your needs in a sun-scorched land and will strengthen your frame. You will be like a well-watered garden, like a spring whose waters never fail." - Isaiah 58:11

"In their hearts humans plan their course, but the Lord establishes their steps." - Proverbs 16:9

"The gatekeeper opens the gate for him, and the sheep listen to his voice. He calls his own sheep by name and leads them out. When he has brought out all his own, he goes on ahead of them, and his sheep follow him because they know his voice." - John 10:3-4

"For the Lord of hosts has planned, and who can frustrate it? And as for His stretched-out hand, who can turn it back?" - Isaiah 14:27

"Behold, God is mighty but does not despise any; He is mighty in strength of understanding." - Job 36:5

"For as the rain and the snow come down from heaven, And do not return there without watering the earth, And making it bear and sprout, And furnishing seed to the sower and bread to the eater; So will My word be which goes forth from My mouth; It will not return to Me empty, Without accomplishing what I desire, And without succeeding in the mater for which I sent it." - Isaiah 55:10-11

"The anger of the Lord will not turn back until He has performed and carried out the purposes of His heart; In the last days will clearly understand it." - Jeremiah 23:20

"And we know that God causes all things to work together for good to those who love God, to those who are called according to His purpose." - Romans 8:28

"Declaring the end from the beginning, and from ancient times the things that are not yet done, saying, My counsel shall stand, and I will do all my pleasure." - Isaiah 46:10

"The Lord is my shepherd; I shall not want. He maketh me to lie down in green pastures: he leadeth me beside the still waters. He restoreth my soul: he leadeth me in the paths of righteousness for his name's sake. Yea, though I walk through the valley of the shadow of death, I will fear no evil: for thou art with me; thy rod and thy staff they comfort me." - Psalm 23:1-4

"For this God is our God for ever and ever: he will be our guide even unto death." - Psalm 48:14

"And the Lord shall guide thee continually, and satisfy they soul in drought, and make fat they bones: and thous shalt be like a watered garden, and like a spring of water, whose waters fail not."
- Isaiah 58:11

"For thus saith, the Lord God; Behold, I even I, will both search my sheep, and seeketh out. As a shepherd seeketh out his flock in the day that he is among his sheep that he is among his sheep that are scattered; so will I seek out my sheep and will deliver them out of all places where they have been scattered in the cloudy and dark day." - Ezekiel 34:11-12

"I will instruct thee and teach thee I n the way which thou shalt go:I will guide thee with mine eye." - Psalm 32:8

Protection

As Christians, we walk by faith and not by sight. We know who our enemy is, and we have faced the one who has come to steal, kill, and destroy. God is our security blanket, and He assures us that He is our Refuge and we have security in Him.

God provides us an umbrella of protection. In our life's journey, we need to make sure that we always have our spiritual umbrella. This spiritual umbrella doesn't stop Satan's from throwing his fiery darts, its just keep those fiery darts from hitting and hurting us. We must always stand under the Umbrella of Jesus. Under His umbrella, we will always be safe.

"No weapon that is formed against thee shall prosper; and every tongue that shall rise against thee in judgment thou shalt condemn. This is the heritage of the servants of the Lord, and their righteousness is of me, saith the Lord." - Isaiah 54:17

"He that dwelleth in the secret place of the most High shall abide under the shadow of the Almighty. I will say of the Lord, He is my refuge and my fortress: my God; in him will I trust. Surely he shall deliver thee from the snare of the fowler, and from the noisome pestilence. He shall cover thee with his feathers, and under his wings shalt thou trust: his truth shall be thy shield and buckler. Thou shalt not be afraid for the terror by night; nor for the arrow that flieth by day. Not for the pestilence that walketh in darness; nor for the destruction that wasteth at noonday. A thousand shall fall at thy side, and ten thousand at thy right hand; but it shall not come nigh thee. Only with thine eyes shalt thou behold and see the reward of the wicked. Because thou hast made the Lord, which is my refuge, even the most High, thy habitation; there shall no evil befall thee, neither shall any plague come nigh they dwelling. For he shall give his angels charge over thee, to keep thee in all thy ways. They shall bear thee up in their hands, lest thou dash thy foot against a stone. Thou shalt tread upon the lion and adder: the young lion and the dragon shalt thou trample under feet. Because he hath set his love upon me, therefore will I deliver him: I will set him on high, because he hath known my name. He shall call upon me, and I will answer him: I will deliver him, and honour him. With long life will I satisfy him, and shew him my salvation." - Psalm 91:1-16.

"God is our refuge and strength, a very present help in trouble." - Psalm 46:1

"Be strong and of a good courage, fear not, nor be afraid of them: for the Lord thy God, he it is that doth go with thee; he will not fail thee, nor forsake thee." - Deuteronomy 31:6

"But the Lord is faithful, who shall stablish you, and keep you from evil." - 2 Thessalonians 3:3

"Fear thou not for I am with thee; be not dismayed; for I am thy God: I will strengthen thee; yea, I will help thee; yea, I will uphold thee with the right hand of my righteousness." - Isaiah 41:10

"Though I walk in the midst of trouble, thou wilt revive me: thou shalt stretch forth thine hand against the wrath of mine enemies, and thy right hand shall save me." - Psalm 138:7

"The name of the Lord is a strong tower: the righteous runneth into it, and is safe." - Proverbs 18:10

"Thy art my hiding place; thou shalt preserve me from trouble thou shalt compass me about with songs of deliverance. Selah." - Psalm 32:7

"But let all those that put their trust in thee rejoice: let them ever shout for joy, because thou defendest them: let them also that love thy name be joyful in thee." - Psalm 5:11

"The Lord shall preserve thee from all evil: he shall preserve thy soul. The Lord shall preserve thy going out and thy coming in from this time forth, and even for evermore." - Psalm 121:7-8

"The God of my rock; in him will I trust: he is my shield and the horn of my salvation, my high tower, and my refuge, my saviour; thou savest me from violence. I will call on the Lord, who

is worthy to be praised: so shall I be saved from mine enemies."
- 2 Samuel 22:3-4

"And we know that all things work together for good to them that love God, to them who are the called according to his purpose."
- Romans 8:28

"We know that whosoever is born of God sinneth not; but he that is begotten of God keepeth himself, and that wicked one toucheth him not." - 1 John 5:18

"What shall we then say to these things? If God be for us, who can be against us?" -Romans 8:31

"And the Lord shall deliver me from every evil work, and will preserve me unto his heavenly kingdom" to whom be glory for ever and ever. Amen." - 2 Timothy 4:18

"Let your conversation be without covetousness; and be content with such things as ye have: for he hath said, I will never leave thee, nor forsake thee." - Hebrews 13:5

"But thou, O Lord, art a shield for me; my glory, and the lifter up of mine head." - Psalm 3:3

"Be merciful unto me, O God, be merciful unto me: for my soul trusteth in thee: yea, in the shadow of thy wings will I make my refuge, until these calamities be overpast." - Psalm 57:1

"The Lord shall fight for you, and ye shall hold your peace." - Exodus 14:14

"I can do all things through Christ which strengtheneth me." - Philippians 4:13

"He shall cover thee with his feathers, and under his wings shalt thou trust: his truth shall be thy shield and buckler." - Psalm 91:4

"The Lord is my light and my salvation; whom shall I fear? the Lord is the strength of my life; of whom shall I be afraid?" - Psalm 27:1

"Every word of God is pure: he is a shield unto them that put their trust in him." - Proverbs 30:5

"I will life up mine eyes unto the hills, from whence cometh my help. My help cometh from the Lord, which made heaven and earth. He will not suffer thy foot to be moved: he that keepeth thee will not slumber." - Psalm 121:1-3

"As for God, his way is perfect: the word of the Lord is tried: he is a buckler to all those that trust in him." - Psalm 18:30

"The Lord redeemeth the soul of his servants: and none of them that trust in him shall be desolate." - Psalm 34:22

"It is better to trust in the Lord than to put confidence in man. It is better to trust in the Lord than to put confidence in princes." - Psalm 118:8-9

"The Lord is good, a strong hold in the day of trouble and he knoweth them that trust in him." Nahum 1:7

"For who is God, save the Lord? and who is a rock, save our God?" - 2 Samuel 22:32

"A thousand shall fall at thy side, and ten thousand at thy right hand; but it shall not come nigh thee." - Psalm 91:7

"The angel of the Lord encampeth round about them that fear him, and delivereth them." - Psalm 34:7

"I have set the Lord always before me: because he is at my right hand, I shall not be moved." - Psalm 16:8

"Many are the afflictions of the righteous; but the Lord delivereth him out of them all." - Psalm 34:19

"I will both lay me down in peace, and sleep: for thou, Lord, only makest me dwell in safety." - Psalm 4:8

"Thou art my hiding place and my shield: I hope in thy word." - Psalm 119:114

GOD'S PROMISES AND ASSURANCES

"Put on the whole armour of God, that ye may be able to stand against the wiles of the devil." - Ephesians 6:11

"And I give unto them eternal life; and they shall never perish, neither shall any man pluck them out of my hand. My Father, which gave them me, is greater than all; and no man is able to pluck them out of my Father's hand. I and my Father are one." - John 10:28-30

"We are troubled on every side, yet not distressed; we are perplexed, but not in despair; Persecuted, but not forsaken; cast down, but not destroyed." - 2 Corinthians 4:8-9

"In whom also we have obtained an inheritance, being predestinated according to the purpose of him who worketh all things after the counsel of his own will." - Ephesians 1:11

"Preserve me, O God: for in thee do I put my trust." - Psalm 16:1

"Thou hast also give me the shield of thy salvation: and thy right hand hath holden me up, and thy gentleness hath made me great. Thou has enlarged my steps under me, that my feet did not slip." - Psalm 18:35-36

"The Lord is my shepherd; I shall not want. He maketh me to lie down in green pastures: he leadeth me beside the still waters. He restoreth my soul: he leadeth me in the paths of righteousness for his name's sake. Yea, though I walk through the valley of the shadow of death, I will fear no evil: for thou art with me; thy rod and thy staff they comfort me." - Psalm 23:1-4

"And the very God of peace sanctify you wholly; and I pray God you whole spirit and soul and body be preserved blameless unto the coming of our Lord Jesus Christ." - 1 Thessalonians 5:23-24

"The Lord is on my side; I will not fear: what can man do unto me?" - Psalm 118:6

"The fear of man bringeth a snare: but whoso putteth his trust in the Lord shall be safe." - Proverbs 29:25

"And even to your old age I am he; and even to hoar hairs will I carry you: I have made, and I bear; even I will carry, and will deliver you." - Isaiah 46:4

"And we know that we are of God, and the whole world lieth in wickedness." - 1 John 5:19

"But ye are a chosen generation, a royal priesthood, an holy nation, a peculiar people; that ye should shew forth the praises of him who hath called you out of darkness into his marvellous light." - 1 Peter 2:9

"And at that time shall Michael stand up, the great prince which standeth for the children of thy people: and there shall be a time of trouble, such as never was since there was a nation even to that same time: and at that time thy people shall be delivered, every one that shall be found written in the book." - Daniel 12:1

"But I will sing of thy power; yea, I will sing aloud of thy mercy in the morning: for thou hast been my defence and refuge in the day of my trouble." - Psalm 59:16

"When thou passest through the waters, I will be with thee; and through the rivers, they shall not overflow thee: when thou walkest through through the fire, thou shalt not be burned; neither shall the flame kindle upon thee." - Isaiah 43:2

"Fear not, little flock; for it is your Father's good pleasure to give you the kingdom." - Luke 12:32

"My brethren, count it all joy when ye fall into divers temptations; Knowing this that the trying of your faith worketh patience." - James 1:2-3

"In whom ye also trusted, after that ye heard the word of truth, the gospel of your salvation: in whom also after that ye believed, ye were sealed with that holy Spirit of promise." - Ephesians 1:13-14

"These things I have spoken unto you, that in me ye might have peace. In the world ye shall have tribulation: but be of good cheer; I have overcome the world." - John 16:33

"And behold, I am with thee, and will keep thee in all places whither thou goest, and will bring thee again into this land; for I will not leave thee, until I have done that which I have spoken to thee of." - Genesis 28:15

"There shall not any man be able to stand before thee all the days of thy life: as I was with Moses, so I will be with thee: I will not fail thee, nor forsake thee." - Joshua 1:5

"Because thous hast kept the word of my patience, I also will keep thee from the hour of temptation, which shall come upon all the world, to try them that dwell upon the earth." - Revelation 3:10

"He will not suffer thy foot to be moved: he that keepeth thee will not slumber." - Psalm 121:3

"For in the time of trouble he shall hide me in his pavilion: in the secret of his tabernacle shall he hide me; he shall set me up upon a rock." - Psalm 27:5

"Deliver me from mine enemies, O my God: defend me from them that rise up against me." - Psalm 59:1

"And Jesus came and spake unto them, saying, "All power is given unto me in heaven and in earth. Go ye therefore, and teach all nations, baptizing them in the name of the Father, and of the Son, and of the Holy Ghost. Teaching them to observe all things whatsoever I have commanded you: and lo, I am with you alway, even unto the end of the world. Amen." - Matthew 28:18-20

"Are they not all ministering spirits, sent forth to minister for them who shall be heirs of salvation?" - Hebrews 1:14

"Finally, my brethren, be strong in the Lord, and in the power of his might. Put on the whole armour of God, that ye may be able to stand against the wiles of the devil. For we wrestle not against flesh and blood, but against principalities, against powers, against the rulers of the darkness of this world, against spiritual wickedness in high places. Wherefore take unto you the whole armour of God, that ye may be able to withstand in the evil day, and having done all, to stand. Stand therefore, having your loins girt about with truth, and having on the breastplate of righteousness. And your feet shod with the preparation of the gospel of peace; Above all, taking the shield of faith, wherewith ye shall be able to quench all the fiery darts of the wicked. And take the helmet of salvation, and the sword of the Spirit, which is the word of God. Praying always with all prayer and supplication in the Spirit, and watching thereunto with all perseverance and supplication for all saints." - Ephesians 6:10-18

"Behold, I give unto you power to tread on serpents and scorpions, and over all the power of the enemy: and nothing shall by any means hurt you." - Luke 10:19

"For God so loved the world, that he gave his only begotten Son, that whosoever believeth in him should not perish, but have everlasting life. For God sent not is Son into the world to condemn the world; but that the world through him might be saved." - John 3:16-17

"Howbeit when he, the Spirit of truth, is come, he will guide you into all truth: for he shall not speak of himself; but whatsoever he shall hear, that shall he speak: and he will shew you things to come." - John 16:13

"But whoso hearkeneth unto me shall dwell safely, and shall be quiet from fear of evil." Proverbs 1:33

"The Lord shall preserve thy going out and thy coming in from this time forth, and even for evermore." - Psalm 121:8

"The Lord hear thee in the day of trouble; the name of the God of Jacob defend thee." Psalm 20:1

"The Lord will preserve him, and keep him alive; and he shall be blessed upon the earth: and thou wilt not deliver him unto the will of his enemies." - Psalm 41:2

"For thou hast been a shelter for me, and a strong tower from the enemy." - Psalm 61:3

"How excellent is thy lovingkindness, O God! therefore the children of men put their trust under the shadow of thy wings." - Psalm 36:7

"One thing have I desired of the Lord, that will I seek after; that I may dwell in the house of the Lord all the days of my life, to behold the beauty of the Lord, and to enquire in his temple." - Psalm 27:4

"When I cry unto thee, then shall mine enemies turn back: this I know; for God is for me." psalm 56:9

"Submit yourselves therefore to God. Resist the devil, and he will flee from you." - James 4:7

www.ingramcontent.com/pod-product-compliance
Lightning Source LLC
Chambersburg PA
CBHW040801150426
42811CB00056B/1125